It Too Shall Pass!

Inspirational Psychology for Self-Ecology!

Long Live the Belief in Life without IF!

Rimaletta Ray, Ph. D

WORKBOOK PRESS LLC
187 E Warm Springs Rd,
Suite B285, Las Vegas, NV 89119, USA

Website: https://workbookpress.com/
Hotline: 1-888-818-4856
Email: admin@workbookpress.com

Ordering Information:
Quantity sales.
Special discounts are available on quantity purchases by corporations, associations, and others.
For details, contact the publisher at the address above.

Library of Congress Control Number:
ISBN-13: 978-1-960752-12-3 (Paperback Version)
978-1-960752-13-0 (Digital Version)

REV. DATE: 13/10/2023

Epigraph

"I want to desperately live

To internalize what can be seen,

To celebrate the unforeseen,

To humanize the irreversible,

And realize the impossible!"

(Alexander Blok in my translation)

Use new technology

for the inspirational,

goodness-instilling

Self-Ecology!

Value Life and Being Alive!

Life is Tough, but I'm Tougher!

I Can Roam Any Terrain with Faith and Confidence in My Vein!

6. *Love Your Life in Its Entire Mass!*

Be in a Hurry

to have Your Say!

You're Here for just a Moment,

Not Even a Day!

So, Embrace Your Life

in its Entire Mass

For it Too

Shall Pass!

Balance Your Life's Surf in Five Dimensions of the Self-Reforming Curve!

*Let Every Sunrise Enlighten Your Path
with a New Enthusiasm Mass!*

(From the collection of Olga Goncharova)

**You Can Roam any Terrain with the
Sunrise in Your Vein!**

Table of Contents

To Be Inspired, Be Self-Inspiring!

Inspiration-Injected Gust

Changes the Mood Very Fast!

For the Reader to First Consider

"Joy-ology"

(Dr. Paul Pearsall)

is My

Phycology!

"Happiness is the Domain of Those that Know."*(Socrates)*

Nothing is Impossible if You make Your Self-Growth Irreversible!

1. Be Sure to Declare,

Self-Induction:

I Love Life

In its Every Form,

And Life Loves Me Back

In Return!

Self-Induction:

My Life is Going on, and It's Great to Have Been Born!

2. Inspirational Psychology for Self-Ecology!

This book is meant to <u>uplift your spirit with the psychologically backed-up inspirational boosters,</u> written in a rhyming form because

"A rhyming word goes better inward. " (*Edgar Cayce*).

But it is not a poetic book of a sentimental mood. It is the reflection of *psychology and language in sync,* or **PSYCHOLINGUISTICS IN ACTION,** aimed at helping you form *an intellectually spiritualized fractal of your being* that we are supposed to be consciously developing in the five levels -*physical, emotional, mental, spiritual, and universal.*

(*www.language-fitness.com / video is in the section Self-Resurrection*)

Following a great, life-forming discovery of *Dr. Benoit Mandelbrot* about *the infinite formation of the fractals and patterns in nature*, I suggest that we focus <u>on the fractal formation of our spiritually eternal nature</u> that we call a soul.

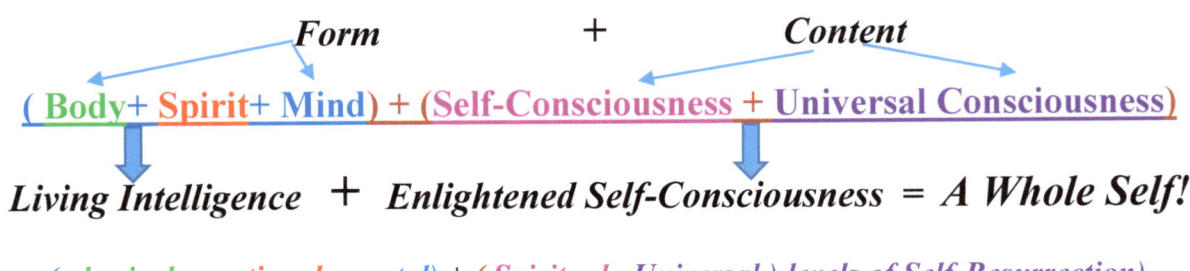

The Fractal of an Intellectually Spiritualized Being:

Form + *Content*

(Body+ Spirit+ Mind) + (Self-Consciousness + Universal Consciousness)

Living Intelligence + *Enlightened Self-Consciousness* = *A Whole Self!*

(*physical ,emotional ,mental*) + (*Spiritual , Universal) levels of Self-Resurrection*).

The book *"It Too Shall Pass!"* like the five books on *the Holistic paradigm of Self-Resurrection*, presented below is featuring each level in a holistic system of self-growth , and it is illustrating this process in an inspirational, poetically rhyming way. With the help of *inspirational, psychologically enhanced boosters and mind-sets* (*the authoritative commands to the brain here*), you will be able to explore each level in an easy to digest, non-intrusive, but persuasive way, up-lifting your spirit and helping you feel unique and more accomplished in it.

There will be very little text re-enforcement in this book - just mostly inspirational mind-sets and boosters to convey the conceptual messages at each level. I do not make them up. They just come to me in a very spontaneous way, once an important concept hits my mind. I jot them down then and there because if I don't do it immediately, they do not enlighten my mind again.

The psychologically charged concepts and the mind-sets at the top and the bottom of the pages also ***rhyme in the mind's twine,*** accentuating the conceptual value of the title and concluding on it. The book can be read consequentially or randomly; it's inspirational purpose will be accomplished ,anyway.

All the boosters are organized ***to illustrate both psychologically and linguistically the five levels of Self-Creation***, presented *in a holistic system* and structured in the fashion of *the Russian dolls*, when *a higher doll embraces all the inside ones*, from bottom to top., forming one structure- *physical, emotional, mental, spiritual, and universal.*

There is no system without the structure!

Life is God + You Pact! So, Act!

3. Self-Growth is Multi-Dimensional!

The five books, presented in the structure below are based on the holistic *Auto-Suggestive Psychology for Self-Ecology* in five philosophical dimensions: *physical, emotional, spiritual, mental, and universal,* featuring the concept of self-growth as the fundamental process in life.

The Holistic Pyramid of Self-Resurrection:

The Levels of Self-Resurrection: / Stages: of Self-Growth / Books, featuring them:

5. *Universal - Super*-Consciousness.	**Self-Salvation**	**"Beyond the Terrestrial!"**
4 *Spiritual - Self-Consciousness*	**Self-Realization**	**"Self-Taming!"**
3. *Mental - Mind*	**Self-Installation**	**" Living Intelligence…"**
2 *Emotional - Spirit*	**Self-Monitoring**	**" Soul-Refining!"**
1. *Physical - Body*	**Self-Awareness**	*"I Am Free to Be the Best…*

"Books are the liberated spirits of men." (Mark *Twain*)

The Fractals of Spiritualized Beings:

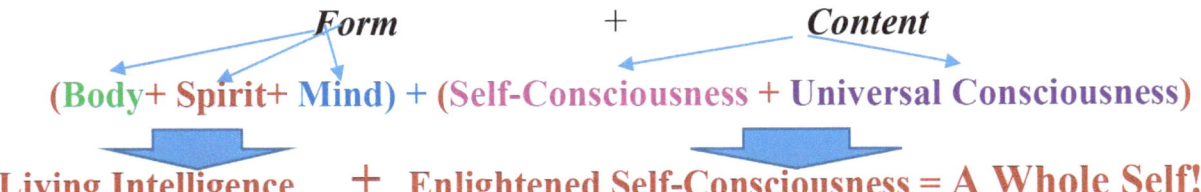

Form   +   Content

(Body+ Spirit+ Mind) + (Self-Consciousness + Universal Consciousness)

Living Intelligence   +   Enlightened Self-Consciousness = A Whole Self!

= A Complete Individual or a Spiritually Refined Fractal of you!)

All five books, as well as the book " **It Too Shall Pass!"** are illustrated with conceptually loaded pictures and psychologically backed-up inspirational boosters. *You can upload them into your smart phone* in the same five levels and organize *the Self-Resurrection* file as your <u>**Self-Help Hypnosis**</u> at hand. <u>Use new technology for Self-Ecology</u>*!*

Follow the Holistic Paradigm to help your Life's Form + Content Rhyme!

4. Make "Joy-ology"
Your Inspirational Psychology!

I'm Happy,

No Matter What!

Happiness is

My Full-Time Job!

Follow the route of Self-Modification without frustration!

Self-Awareness ➡ **Self- Monitoring** ➡ **Self-Installation**

➡ **Self-Realization** . ➡ **Self-Salvation**

(Physical, emotional, mental, spiritual, universal level of Self-Resurrection)

Happiness is the Process of Self-Resurrection - Section by Section!

5. Don't Be Death-Bound!

To Begin with, process the psychic energy of your inner peace through the *physical, emotional, mental, spiritual, and universal grids.*

Your psychological courtesy for life is in their widths.

(For more on Self-Resurrection in five levels, forming a fractal of a spiritually intellectualized being, check out my five books, presented in the video

----

"To stay above the ground, not under the ground,

Don't be death-bound!

Don't kill your dream, your love and passion

In a crowd-stereotyped fashion!

Put your mind and heart in a joint kindness act,

Don't be negatively stuck!

You have this chance, but Once!

Don't Be in a Rush to Become

Biological Trash!

6. Many Die a Senseless Death!

*Many die a very senseless death,**

<u>*They must have lived in the darkest depth,*</u>

In an ignorant haze

Of a blind money chase!

Or they've wasted their lives

<u>*On drugs, fun, sex, and the fights,*</u>

Or they were part of a rabid mob

That lives like a retaliating snob

That craves to get even and to rob

<u>*You of the light of God!*</u>

In the aftermath of such a life,

What for is there to survive?

Reluctantly, they live

<u>*And senselessly they die,*</u>

Enormously relived

<u>*That they at all lived!*</u>

Release the Fear of Death
To Be on the Path of the Life's Fest!

7. *"Excessive Happiness" is not a Sizable Bliss, It's an Earned Mind-Release!*

Your Evolutionary Goal:

Internalize Your Emotions, but Externalize the Mind! Be One of a Kind!

If you want to have happiness in its might,
Enjoy life at every site!

It's Not Enough to Be Special; Become Exceptional!

If You Want to Be Happy, just Be –
Like God and Me!

8. Life-Forming is in Knowing and Character Re-forming!

Don't just survive! Keep bettering your life!

For centuries, life has been a cruel game of money-chasing and money-raising, of wars and territorial quarrels, of aggressive international relationships and treacherous private deals, of betrayed love and ruined family stuff. *Isn't it enough?*

When Will We Start Loving Life?

Life is Tough, but I'm Tougher!

I Can Roam Any Terrain with Faith and Confidence in My Vein!

<u>Book Incentive</u>

Our
"Civilized
<u>Barbarism!"</u>

"There is too much talk about heaven because too many people made hell out of themselves." (Sadhguru)

Let's Turn Our Life-Deforming Barbarism into Life-Forming Fanatism!

1. *Our "Civilized Barbarism!"* (Carl Yung)

We live in the country of "civilized barbarism",

Seen in the culture, politics, and a fake socialism!

Like robots on the remote control,

We are marching forward to an abyss of the moral!

Any sphere of life is bureaucratically smeared,

There is no heart or understanding in it!

Intellectual barbarians of education

Are heartless machines in the digital reformation!

The urges of the insatiable guts

Smear tons of minds and hearts!

The TV shows and news up-dates

Are filled up with cooking debates!

The TV injections of the religious insulin

Into the social blood stream

Can hardly change

The common blindness range!

How can an independent intellect survive

In this barbarian thrive

To get, to sell, and to repel

Any intellectually charged individual cell?

Our malignant social tumor

Has become the point of the world's rumor!

    We need to nib it in the bud,

    And stop its growth in our poisoned gut!

Many American values are long gone,

They are not even in any reform!

    The piece of ice in our hearts and talks

    Turns out to be just a drink on the rocks!

There is no leader with a constructive vision

To take up the social relay mission!

    Dollar-efficacy, mental inertia, and moto-rism

    Form the American "civilized barbarism!"

The culture is chronically sick,

Alienated by the collective stereotype bleak!

    The impartiality of the American Law

    Is with the real justice at war!

There is also a lot of talk

About a new Enlightenment walk,

    But on the path of the spiritual enhancement,

    There is no visible advancement!

The Homo Sapience consciousness

Is the instrument of animal unconsciousness!

Multiple obstacles in finances,

Doubled with temptations, trials, and vices,

Stem from the moral's decay

That is at the country's bay

People prostitute themselves for the money power

With a satanically diabolic devour

The" collective unconscious" of our youth

Is unable to inflame the revolutionary fuse!

Thus, we continue to falter along the way,

Full of commonly blind dismay!

Does it seem to be a true American Dream?

So, why don't we recharge our NEW magnetic rim

And start changing our social scene!

Then the information technology revolution

Will not be polluting our spiritual constitution

And the universally spiritual "mrak "(darkness)

Will turn into a one-way evolutionary track!

Not to Be Lost on Earth,

Try Not to Lose Your Self-Worth!

2. We're Not Getting Better; We're Getting Bitter!

We are not getting better,

We are getting bitter

When we see cruelty and injustice,

Still unstopped with a Veto!

There is a lot of religious yearning,

But human life is still burning!

When and where

Will we start to beware

That our moral steep

Is still on a guilt trip?

The words "placid" and "serene"

Are rapidly getting obscene

We still wonder, "Which are the ways

For the Christ consciousness to surface?"

The reasons for that are immense,

But the acts of reasoning are in defense!

We, obviously, need to start

Making kinder a human heart

We still need to release

A lot of anger disease!

        We have to un-bitter

        A lot of emotional litter!

We cannot give up

Even on the tiny stuff

        That's left in you, your brother, and the son

        Anyone, who stretches his hand for a moto-gun!

Let us give ourselves a conscience bite

And stand up for it very tight!

        There is always hope

        Even for the most merciless dope!

There is always some Sun

In a puddle of dirty fun!

        All we need to see

        Is the soul that has no glee!

But there is always a good grain

In some deeply buried plain

        Where we can plant a seed

        For some golden sand to proceed

Then, this soul will start to shine

Even if it's tied up with a course twine.

All we need to add

Is some more golden sand!

Thus, we'll build a castle, grain by grain,

On a lost soul's terrain!

The dirty foam will subside

Finally, aside;

And a lost soul

Will feel consoled!

" Communication is a Mutual Psychological Impact of people on each other."

(V. M. Behterev -" Mysteries of a Human Brain")

Every human contact is a responsibility!

Being Godly in a Godless World is Our Life's First True Award!

3. Every Bad Guy is Worth a Try!

I declare, every bad, white of black, guy

Is worth a try,

Every bastard

Can be reframed faster

If we give him a

Chance

To reform himself , at least,

Once!

Even the one with a deadly gun

Can be re-done!

Thus, his or her soul

Will be consoled

He or she'll go in the right direction

For his or her Soul's Resurrection!

"Life is an Hour Long", but it shouldn't be gone without your having sung Your Sworn Song!

"Life is Going on, and it is Worth Your Having Been Born!"

4. We Hear a Lot of Buzz about the Free Us!

We hear a lot of buzz

About the free us!

Freedom of choice, of speech, of religion,

But are they all in a visible region?

"The collective psyche's" farce

Is indoctrinated in our human mass.

Minds are channeled

By the mass media channel!

The Prometheus of the mind

Is carrying the torch trying to find

A glowing spiritual spark

In the human mass that's still very dark .

A true mind expansion

Is at the grips of a blind repulsion.

The electronic mind's pollution

Is getting into the human minds' fusion.

With a general heart -staleness

And a huge spiritual laziness!

A lot of creative energy is being used

Mostly to infuse a dollar fuse

That is not used to clean up the whack

On the society's evolutionary track

On which every inch of our collective brain

Is bereft with the digital information rain!

So, let's get off our robotic ass

And become again kind and caring us!

Be Kind to the Unkind; Be One of a Kind!

Put your Mind and Heart in Sync.

Feel but Think!

There is Always Room for a Noble Deed

if you have a Kind Heart , Indeed!

(Upload your smart phone with a new inspirational tone!)

Only then Could we Put our Human Pace

in Sync with Evolution in Time and Space!

5. Our March Forward in the Year 2020 and Onward!

Our march for-ward

For centuries and on-ward

Has been filled with wrong turns,

Backsliding, and military burns!

But taken in its grand sweep,

It has been a march forward, indeed ,

In every dimension

And without any exception!

However, the cosmic realm of objectivity

Remains to be seen in Christ's nativity!

Here comes a deadly catch

Of the humanity's split at large!

— — — — — — —

Christ made a strong case

For the centuries of evolutionary waste

In the spiritual dimension,

As was the initial God's intention

For when it comes to Arts and Science,

We marched forward with some godly appliance.

But on the infinity's divine plane,

We are devoid of the progress vein!

A lot of ruthless wars, religious discords, and doubt,

Material greed, destruction, and disbelief count!

They are still filling up the humanity's way

With much suffering and religious dismay!

True, our digital potential for creation

Is in the abundance formation!

Gifts are embedded in the human mind,

All we need to do is to try and find

How to unite the human hoard,

Into one fundamentally universal fort,

Strong in its firm determination

To secure the Earth preservation!

For in the vast universal spell, our unique human cell

Is on the track of the cosmic expel!

Due to our uncontrolled consumption,

We are prone to total self-destruction

So, let's synchronize our technological march

With a new spiritual retouch

Of the consideration for the Mother Earth

And Christ's Consciousness true rebirth!

Our Human Essence is in the Spiritual Renaissance!

"Every saint has the past; every sinner has the future."

(An Ancient saying)

Use technology for your Self-Ecology!

(Upload your smart phone with the mind-sets of a new

inspirational tone!)

The Longer we Live, the Clearer we See that Knowing is a Bottomless Sea!

6. Recovery or Self-Recycling

A real recovery for me

Is the self-recycling of my inner glee.

Love becomes love in every vein,

And life is worth living again!

But I must be bold

To fit into a new life's mold!

Only then can I overcome

My inner insufficiency scum!

If I relapse again,

I'll command to my new vein,

"Be nice and beautiful and beware,

There are eyes and ears everywhere!"

People always judge,

So, you should not oblige

Their thirst for your emotional blood

With your inner mud

Keep it to yourself

And boost your every cell with the thinking spell!

"Right is Might!" *(Richard W. Wetherill)*

I'm Always Life-Abreast; I Am on the Spiritual Quest!

"Every life is a conscious search for oneself."

(Leo Vygotsky" Psychology of Art")

What Are You Here for?

(All the pictures of the rocks are from my collection" Consciousness is in Everything!"

The Know-How of My Inspirational "WOW"!

The Auto- Suggestive Injections for Good Mood Projections

(Mind-Sets against Upsets)

The Self- Inductive Rhythming changes a

Personal Algorithm! of your life driving!

Life Production needs a Lot of Self- Induction!

<u>Section One</u>

In Each Space-Time Phase,

You Need to Balance Your Life's Base!

"Time is Not Money! Time is Life!"

(Sadhguru)

1. Help Yourself to Love Life More;

Dear friends, the inspirational ,psychologically enhanced boosters and programming verses on the pages of this book are the continuation of my first book, called "*Emotional Diplomacy*, "inspired by the life-ruining *September 11, 2001* events that have changed our lives.

The inspirational programs in this book are meant *to help you uplift your spirit and make yourself strong in it!* They were written most spontaneously in a desperate effort to help my daughter *reprogram herself for life* after that horrible day in which she had most miraculously survived.

One day, while driving to college, I discovered that my thinking was being framed into some inspirational boosters that were essay-structured in the *Introduction, Body*, and *Conclusion* rhyming way. It was a surprising revelation, especially after I realized that my first booster did have a *wakening up effect* on my daughter when I just jotted it down for her to see on our kitchen board. Surprisingly, I kept writing them every day, without pressing my ideas on her, just giving her the chance to read them and experience *the epiphany of life-programming* in them.

The first boosters were very simple, even primitive, but they never stopped hitting my mind ever since. With these *inspirational boosters coming to me as the help from the Above*, I also started backing up my life-overwhelmed students who are thirsty for support of self-belief at these very tough times of ours. Since you have taken this book into your hands, you most certainly, have read a lot of self-help books that take you on a ride for a self-discovery. *This book is different!*

That's Your Life's Sustaining Core!

2. Man is Self-Consciousness at Work - Not an Empty Talk!

I am not loading you up here with the pages of psychologically charged information or any personal stories to prove the messages involved. I am not trying to change you, either. I think we are tired of the self-help books that speak of the same problems in the same way. Affirmations stop working at some point, too.

I am just trying to inspire you, to uplift you to new <u>universal, spiritual, mental, emotional, and physical heights</u> with the help of the mind-sets that rhyme in the mind's twine. Inspirational boosters result in the relaxation response that calls for *the action of thought!*

Self-Inspiration is the Salvation!

It's easier to remember the rhyming lines that resonate in your mind and heart. In our hard-wired present-day life, we all need <u>to develop the ability to regulate our emotional pendulum,</u> not to let it swing too much to the left (*the negative swing*) or too much to the right (*the positive swing),* enhanced with excitement, too much fun, hyper emotions, and exaltation.

We need **to optimize our mental and emotional reactions,** keep them away from the stressful extremes. We absolutely must teach ourselves the basics of EMOTIONAL DIPLOMACY that is indispensable for a full realization of our lives. Emotional diplomacy is **the ART OF BALANCING** yourself for life in its *physical, emotional, mental, spiritual, and universal* realms in sync with life itself.

"One can't live his life without changing his Mind-Sets Stuff." *(V. Behterev)*

3. Holistic Personal Evolution is the Solution!

The process of **SELF-CREATION** is based on the same laws of life in which the chaos of destruction is followed by the order of construction that is evolving in levels, from the lowest to the highest ones. The inner chaos that we are all experiencing at one time or another needs to be turned to <u>a constructive order at the *physical, emotional, mental, spiritual, and universal levels.*</u> When this process is continuous, conscious, and rational, we feel good with ourselves, and we are more pleasant to deal with for other people. That's why when we do good things, we feel balanced and content. **<u>In fact, we become godly in the form and content</u>**! Life gets synchronized with the Universal Intelligence .*"Our consciousness is a chaotic informational phenomenon , based on the processes of order. "* Dmitriy Vereshchagin)

Stay aboard! Tune Yourself up to the Station God!

Interestingly, our morals and ethics are secondary here. The point is, to create a **NEW YOU** is a beneficial and explainable process from the point of view of the laws of the Universe that is developing from simple to the complex, from entropy to new energy of life construction, *taking us to new levels of actionable thought evolution,* one step at a time.

So, when we are leading lives in this evolutionary way, destroying the lower realms of self-growth and creating the new, higher ones consciously, we are building up our lives in sync with the universal laws of creation. We feel energized, enthusiastic, goal-oriented , self-realizing, and happy. We feel accomplished and enlightened. Naturally, when we are not on the self-growth path and are not bothered by consciously moving toward higher levels of self-creation, we <u>fall into a disbalance at the *physical, emotional ,mental, spiritual, and universal levels</u>,* and therefore, we feel depressed and life-disillusioned. Change your soul's range in every level consequentially and continuously!

Choreograph Yourself in Every Cell!

4. Self-Help Psychology for Inner Ecology!

This book is based on *the auto-suggestive injections in the form of the inspirational boosters and mind-sets with the psychological background.* They rhyme and are structured in a conceptual order, serving as the AUTO-SUGGESTIVE PSYCHOLOGY for SELF-ECOLOGY! For a more fundamental philosophy of managing your life in five dimensions, you can check the five books on *Self-Resurrection* on my website (*See www. language-fitness.com.- the Self-Resurrection section)*

The purpose of this book is just to nail into your head the idea that you are the only person on Earth able to boost your spirit, cleanse it of any depressive wart , and fill it up with the flying thought! You can read the book from any part or open it randomly *to boost the spirit and inspire yourself in any department of your life (physical, emotional, mental, spiritual, universal*) at any time and in any place. Find the necessary support in the level that you consider to be the weakest with you and *upload the mind-sets that resonate most with you into your smart phone* . Have them at hand when your mood sags and you need to up-lift your spirit with *a reality-boosting in-put.*

Inspirationally re-form your reality's de-form!

The rhyming boosters are illustrated with the pictures of the rocks that have conceptual images in them. They are all authentic, and they are from my collection, called *"Consciousness is Everywhere and in Everything!* Each rock was found on the ocean shore, and every time I find the rock *"talking to me"* among the infinite number of the silent ones, they prove to me that the entire connection of life in its every form is our UNIVERSAL UNIFORM. It means that *the mental projection of your new digital self should be in sync with your personal cell!* Be true to your inner Merkabah and delete *the mind minus heart* abracadabra! Put the heart and mind in sync! Feel but think!

The Choice is Yours; You are the Boss!

To Balance Yourself,

You Need to Program Your Cells!

The chaos of our past lives is directing us to the order of the present and the future that is mutual!

We are Still Very Young in the Evolutionary Plan!

5. Life is Me! Life is My Philosophy!

The Main Auto-Induction for Life-Production:

I Accept My Life

in its Entire Mass

For it Too

Shall Pass!

(Use the Inspirational Mind-Sets against Upsets!)

I'm My Best Friend;

I'm My Beginning and My End!

Section Two

The Auto-Suggestive Meditation for Inner Consideration!

The Vectors of Time and Space
Form Your Cells' Interface.

1. Self-Induction in the Time and Space Function

I suggest you do a simple, but very effective **AUTO-SUGGESTIVE MEDITATION,** *programming you for a positive action and boosting your spirit* at every step of the Holistic Paradigm, in this book presented from the above – *(universal, spiritual, mental, emotional, and physical levels).*

We all bless our loved ones and the people that were good to us. We bless ourselves with the cross blessing when finishing our praying. But *the cross is not just a religious symbol* that we put on ourselves for a divine protection. It's also *the scientific symbol of the unity of yours with the world across! Dr. Sam Gazarkh in his "World-ology"* writes,

"The vectors of time and space are forming our inner interface"

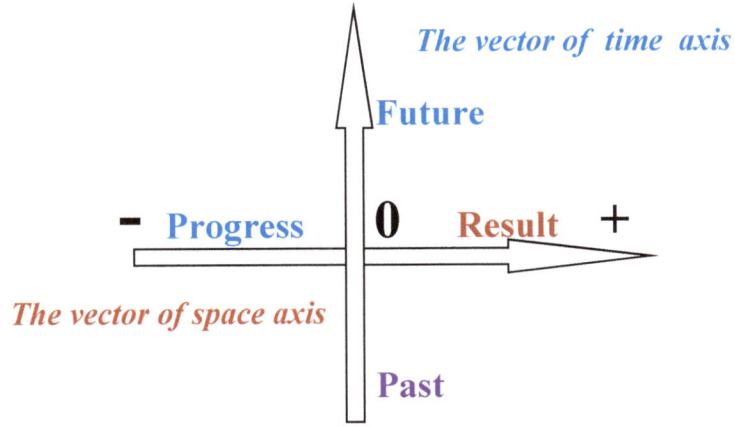

So, let's take into consideration this scientific observation and complete the inspirational self- boosting on the ladder of *the Universal level first.* There are two main forms of meditation *- active and passive.* In P**assive Meditation,** we are quieting the body processes and calming the mind, *transcending into the vastness of the Above realms of the extra-terrestrial dimensions.* My favorite ones are *the Transcendental Meditation by Dr. John Hagelin and Yogi Meditation by Sadhguru*

In my Active Meditation, **you are actively programming the mind and the body cells** by tranquilizing them through **the authoritative, mind+ body friendly commands ,** training the body to listen to its boss - **the MIND.** I suggest you conduct self-inducting with the help of a very simple, but very effective, relaxing, and invigorating meditation below . Note ,please, your aware attention should be focused on your cells!

The Auto-Inductive Meditation is conducted at the cellular level!

In my five books on the *Auto-Suggestive Psychology for Self-Ecology*, I describe different forms **of Active Auto-Suggestive Meditation**, *or Self-Help Inducting.* We can draw the parallel here between the <u>five levels of self-growth</u> (*physical, emotional, mental, spiritual, and universal_*) with *five fingers on our hands* that when squeezed in a fist add willpower to our character wings. Your willpower needs to be constantly activated inwardly, too, ***through your authoritative commands to the cells*** that need constant programming and re-programming according to the digital biologist *Dr. Bruce Lipton.*

Self-inducting is like pumping the emotional gas to your spirit.

The spirit forms the most important link between the **MIND** and **the HEART** that must be in sync. Unfortunately, in our technologically enhanced lives , we became **heart - mind disconnected ,** and I think that this disconnection results into many social and private problems that we face, demanding we restore our ***intellectually spiritualized inner store.***

Form   +   Content

(Body+ Spirit+ Mind) + (Self-Consciousness + Universal Consciousness)

" When You are Whole, You Become Holy"

(Deepak Chopra)

2. Embrace Your Life in its Time and Space. They are Your Life's Base!

Five fingers on our hands are amazingly linked to the five main action indications in every language: **the past, the present, and the future,** as well as **the process and the result** of our life actions with **the zero position,** indicating the **Soul's Balance** in the mathematical, space-time equation. Use your" **active imagination**" *(Carl Yung)* for inner elation.

Breathing through the tips of the fingers , we establish the time-space linking, *training the body to live in the inseparable unity of the mind and the heart.*

I conduct **the Active Auto-Suggestive Meditation** with my students in the middle of the lecture, when I feel that their attention is slacking. They love it!

Thus, their aware attention is not in retention!

Their aware attention gets charged with *new conscious energy* , and they continue studying/ perceiving my instructional in-put in a much more productive way.

" Be conscious! Consciousness mobilizes!" (*Neale. Donald Walsch)*

I recommend you do *the Auto-Suggestive meditation in time -space* after each step on the inspirational ladder of Self-Resurrection ,presented in this book below, level by level.

Please, note that when we **put the central three fingers together** and make the pinkie and the thumb go widespread to the sides, we ,actually get the cross that is also the philosophic sign, representing the two vectors – **the vector of time** and **the vector of space** By the way, the body of a standing man with his arms ,stretched to the sides has the same structure.

Be Every Day a New Human Being!

3. Consciously Connect Your Human Force to the Universe!

So, by the <u>Vector of Time</u>, we have - (*the central finger-* the **present**) ; *the ring finger – ***the-past*** ; *the index finger-***the future**). By the <u>Vector of Space,</u> we are moving from **the pinkie** (*absence of result in space*) **to the thumb** (*the result finger*).Thus, we are moving from **minus (-)** to the **plus (+) of our life , or to its full realization**. No wonder we show the thumb , in any language,   when things are great.

Vector of time

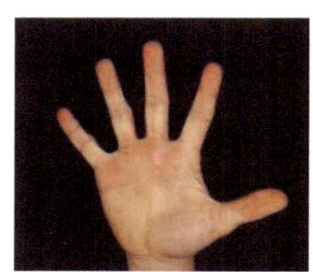 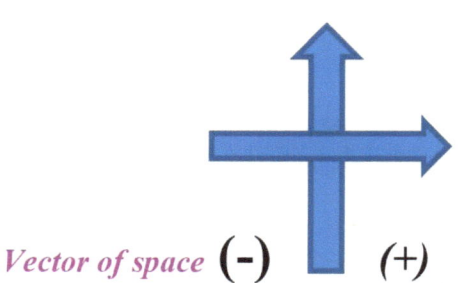

Vector of space **(-)** **(+)**

The Active Auto-Suggestive Meditation for Cells Invention!

The process of self-inducting is inseparable with *consciously channeled breathing* because the energy of a human body is tightly connected with a person's self-consciousness. The main energy flow ,from head to too, streaming up and down the spine, is the main channel that connects us to the Universe through the **AUTO-ANTENNAON** on the top of a head.

 I write about the necessity to develop the **AUTO-MEDIA** perceptive **skill** in all my books on Self-Resurrection because *this skill become the priority at the digital time of our evolution. We need to be consciously connected to <u>the Universal Intelligence that we call God!</u>*

Enlighten Your Being with New, Technologically Enhanced, Thinking, Feeing, Acting, and Seeing!

4. Establish a Psychic Protection against Evil Injection! *(Part One)*

First **rub your hands vigorously and shake them off several times** to cleanse the energy that your hands have accumulated during the day. **Do conscious self-inducting , breathing through the tips of your fingers. Start from the left hand.** Put both hands, with the open palms up on your knees.

1) Start breathing with **the pinkie on the left hand** *(your life in process)* with the eyes closed saying inwardly the induction below. Breathe in. saying inwardly the first part of the induction, **make a pause**, **focusing on the heart's beat -21-21-21,** and finish the induction, breathing out , saying the second part s of the induction slowly, **in sync with your cells.**

They accumulate the mental energy together with your breath.

Channel the air stream up the left arm, the shoulder, making the pause in the heart . Next, channel inwardly the breath down the right shoulder and the arm **to the tip of the pinkie on the right hand** , breathing out through it. After doing the meditation a couple of times, you will literally fel the breeze at the tips of your fingers when you breathe out.

Focus on the air flow consciously , lovingly, and characterfully.

Inwardly, program yourself, saying to yourself, *visualizing your cells in the entire body* follow your breath and the mind's commands. Slowly breath e out, focusing on the induction for a few seconds before going to the next finger.:

Life in going on *(breathe in)* ***Pause*** / **and it's beautiful!** *(breathe out)*

2) **Next,** breathe in through **the ring finger on the left hand** *(your past life)* **) – Pause at the heart!** - (breathe out though **the ring finger on the right hand),** channeling the breath in the same fashion-.up the left arm, the shoulder, making a pause in the heart and visualizing the stream of your breath going to the right shoulder, down the right arm ,to the ring

finger on the right hand. the right shoulder, finishing the breath at the tip of the finger.

I forgive myself_(*breathe in*) - Pause - all my past mistakes. (*breathe out)*

3) Breathe in through the central finger (*your everyday life)*) – Pause , focusing on the heart -**21-21-21** Breathe out though the central finger on the right hand, channeling the breath as is described above.

I live *(breathe in*) - Pause - consciously! *(breathe out)*

4) Breathe in though **the index finger** (*your life in the future*)) – **Pause** (breathe out through the index finger of the right hand) *Visualize what you are planning to do.*

I will do_*(breathe in)* - Pause - whatever I plan to! *(breathe out)*

5) Breathe in through **the thumb of the left hand** *(the result of your life)* – **Pause** – *(breathe out through the thumb of the right hand.)* Envision what you have done that day, week, month ,etc.

I have already_*(breathe in)* - Pause - done a lot!" *(breathe out)*

Open your eyes and *say authoritatively out loud the mind-sets below*, breathing in deeply through the right palm; breathe out though the left palm.

Relax for half a minute or a minute, without breathing Do the same active inducting, starting with the thumb of the right hand , the one you finished your self-inducting with.

Life's Going on, (*Breathe in*) *and it's Great in My Own Form!* (*Breathe out*)

5. Use Your "Active Imagination" against any Frustration! *(Part Two)*

Next, breathe in and out in the opposite direction ,starting with **the thumb of the right hand** and breathing out though **the thumb of the left hand**. Continue breathing in the same fashion through all the fingers: **the pointing finger, the central finger, the ring finger, and the pinkie** in the opposite succession, using the same, slightly modified text

The meditation will end with the pinkie of the left hand, from which it started, **reminding us that life is the process.** A pinkie is the finger of the process of life that we are in. Surprisingly, in any language the verb tense of the prime use and importance is always the one that defines the process of the action at the present moment.

The importance of NOW is in every action. WOW!

Don't forget to channel the energy with the help of **AWARE ATTENTION** , channeling it up the arm, through the chest, down the other arm, out through the corresponding finger. **Don't forget to make a loving pause at the heart.** Breathe in and out slowly and mindfully. Envision your latest accomplishments and plans. . *You are programming the citizens of your body –* your cells in time and space.

Embrace them inwardly with grace , embrace!

1) **The thumb** *(the result of your life that day, week, month, year.* **Envision it!**

I have already*(breathe in)* – Pause - accomplished a lot!.*(breathe out)*

2) The index finger – (*Envision what you are going to do)*

I will do *(breathe in)*) – Pause - even more !*(breathe out)*

3) The central finger – *(Your everyday life)*

Because I live *(breathe in)*) – Pause - consciously! *(breathe out)*

4) The ring finger – *(Your past life)*

Because I forgive myself *(breathe in)*) –Pause -all my past mistakes.*(breathe out)*

5) The pinkie – *(Your life in the Now!- the process of your life)*

My life is going on *(breathe in)*) – Pause - and it is beautiful!"
(breathe (out)

Concluding **the AUTO-SUGGESTIVE Meditation** open your eyes and say authoritatively out loud the mind-sets below, breathing in deeply **through the right palm**; breathe out **though the left palm**. After you have practiced such breathing a couple of times, you will literally feel a slight breeze at the tips of your fingers when you breathe out, and even from your palms. *This Auto-Suggestive meditation seems to be very simple, but it is incredibly powerful and invigorating*.

You can use practically use any mind-set from any of my books. *Upload in those of them that resonate with you most into your smart phone.* Be sure to sort them out for the purpose that you need. in a special file. They will become your helping hand in any upsetting situation. You can also make up your own boosters, but they must rhyme. *"The rhyming word goes better inward!"* (Edgar Cayce)

I'm My Best Friend; (Breathe in);

I'm My Beginning and My End! (Breathe out)

6. Create a Mental Binder for the Inspirational Reminder!

Auto-Induction for Life-Production:

I Embrace My Life

in its Entire Mass

for it Too

Shall Pass!

(Use technology for your consciously sustained Self-Ecology)

Upload your phone with a new inspirational tone!

Life is Me;

Life is My Philosophy!

7. To Spiritually Survive, Follow the Three Main Rules of Life -

"Reject - Resist – Reform!"

Only then can you put on the

"Intellectually Spiritualized"

Uniform!

To follow God and to be happy in life, no matter what, is not just to be kind, do good things, frequent the church, and pray when life gets sour. It also means to TAME YOURSELF - *physically, emotionally, mentally, spiritually, and universally -* and refrain from thinking, saying, feeling, and doing bad things to yourself and others.

"Bad habits have a good tendency – either you kill them, or they kill you!" (Albert Einstein)

Nothing is Impossible if You Make your Inner Change Irreversible!

The First Recall for Your Mood's Fall!

Uplift
Your Spirit
Every Minute!

Don't Tag Along for too Long!

Use the Auto-Suggestive Meditation for Inner Elation!

Your *Life's Bliss* is in Appreciating the Power of *What IS!*

The Beauty of Lie is in Being Alive!

Self-Consciousness, based on Self-Knowledge is forming Life-Storage!

1. "To Be or Not to Be?"

(To the sceptics of life, " You'd Better Live, Not Survive!)

In life, there are a lot of tasks

When inner Hamlet asks,

> **"To Be or not to Be?'**

> **Is there sense in life for me?**

The wind, the clouds, and the sky

Reply, "You'd better fly!"

> **The Moon, in echo to them,**

> **Says in tandem,**

> **"Don't ever swoon your stem!"**

The Earth reminds of the birth

And makes you not forget,

> **"It's not your time, yet!"**

For centuries on end

The answer is a bet!

> **For there's still no expense**

> **For life's suspense!**

So, the logic that I mention

Is still in the retention

Of life's declarative review,

<u>*TO BE and no other view!*</u>

"Self-Salvation is in understanding the sense of your life." (Anton Chekov)

Every Inspirational Booster in this book is reflecting this or that psychological angle of <u>Self-Resurrection</u>, presented in the poetic form in five dimensions of life consequentially – from top to bottom -

Universal, Spiritual, Mental, Emotional, and Physical .

The main engine of life is faith - the faith in God, yourself, your goal, your potential, love and life itself.

<u>Inspiration + Elation + Concentration = New Life's Formation!</u>

Make Your Heart Smart and the Mind Kind!

<u>**Be One of a Kind!**</u>

Life is Going on, and it's Time for Self-Reform!

2. Let Me Have My Say!

Let me have my Say

In my own way!

Let me sing my swan song

Without any reform!

I need to un-

load

My mind's

load;

I need to create

My own self-realized fate!

So, follow the

Way

Of my spiritual sur-

vey!

Don't be a technological clone!

(Upload your smart phone with a new inspirational tone!)

Raise the Spiritual Bar for your Inner Spa!

3. Read My Poetic Oblong

Read my poetic oblong

And get inwardly strong!

Put on a smile as a shield

Against any one's negative field!

Soften your heart,

And leave its wounds uncut!

Secure your mental space holes

For the boldest goals!

Fly in your mind to the Moon,

And don't you ever swoon!

Any sad story-set is but an element

In the Universal Life's Web!

So be sure to say,

Without any inner dismay,

"Everything I have, I do, I see

Gladdens Me!

And you know what,

Happiness is my Full-Time Job!"

Enjoy Your Lifetime, Do Not Whine!

4. Join Me in My Plea!

I have an urge to write

About my life's bite,

About the wonders of the Above

And the blows of the Out;

About the secrets of the ups

And the stories of the about;

About my inspirational twists

And the people's resists,

About the ins of the heart,

And the outs of the emotions, at that;

About the human ocean

And the branches of the Life Tree,

About   him , her, and Thee!

About my self-pity bursts

And many tearful thirsts;

About the steel of a human will

And the pettiness of its weaknesses' seal!

So, join me in my spiritual plea

And add to it some of your own glee!

Live in the Mania of Life's Superior Criteria!

5. I'm Still Up the Hill!

In our time-limited file,

There are two directions of the lifestyle:

Up the hill,

Or down the hill

Which is your direction still?

I declare to self-reveal,

"I'm not going down the hill!"

I walk, I crawl, I move up the hill,

Even if I kneel!

My spirit is upward rolling,

It's not falling!

I'm young, no matter what,

The age is my life's reward!

Life is Going on, and It's Worth My Having Been Born!

6. The Age Booster!

(Pick the age you were at your best and induct yourself with it)

I am 27...

And not a day more!

I am as young,

As ever before!

I am dynamic, as ever,

I am sluggish - Never!

I was, I am, and I will be young

Forever!

It's Not How Long We Live,

It's How We Live!

7. Learn to Savor Life!

We savor life and feel its sweetness

Only when we are through with its bitterness!

But life is sweet

In its every beat!

It does not speed,

If we are upbeat,

Nor does it sit,

If we are down on the depression seat.

So, do we need the skills of a wizard

To live in unison with it?

Why not love life in you

While you are not yet the mildew?

Let's not get involved

Only with the problem of What?

-"What should I do?"

-"What do you want to?"

-"What have you done"?

-"What have you accomplished, son?"

These questions upset

And spiritually off-set.

They push us back

On the life-stress track!

The questions of How?

Are much more connected with Now!

The answers to them

Are in the curves of every life's stem.

We just need

To be wiser and more upbeat

So, let's be with life in awe

And want it more and more!

For if we believe, we receive,

And that's the fun of any problem's outcome!

I love life in its every form, and life loves me back in return!

The Philosophy of "Life is a Bitch and then you Die" isn't for Those who Want to Fly!

8. Self-Boosters at Hand

Auto-Induction:

In My Everyday Life,

I Manage to Survive

With a Smile on My Face

And an Ever-Unbreakable Faith!

I'm tough, resilient, and self-reliant!

I'm One of a Kind!

There wasn't, there isn't, there won't ever be

Anyone like Me!

So, Be Soul-Attractive and Overly Active!

Practice Detachment

from the Negative Fun Attachment!

9. I Slow Up My Slow Down!

My bio-state is great,

I never ask for energy rebate!

I have a meditative fest,

I fill myself up with life zest!

It flows in and out

So, I can sprout

The shoots of the connection

Between the body and spirit in reflection.

No hurry, no haste,

No worry, no waste!

Thus, I defy the gravity of my age

With a peaceful and graceful rage!

Nor do I ever yell or frown,

I slow up my slow down!

The Main Self-Induction:

I'm My Best Friend.

I'm My Beginning and My End!

(End of my Auto-Suggestive Preamble)

Introduction to the Inspirational Self-Induction

(Main Parts of the Book in its Five Levels Inspirational Nook)

We're changing the Software of Our Lives!

(The Five Main Steps of Self-Resurrection in Psychologically Charged Boosters and Mind-sets against Upsets!)

Use New Technology for Self-Ecology!

Your Memory is Your Life's Inventory!

"The Rhyming Word goes Better Inward!"

Beauty is Me ; Beauty is My Philosophy!

Every Moment of WOW! is Now!

1. Chaos and Order

"Pay attention and gain understanding."(Proverbs 4:1)

Chaos and order constitute life,

Both are essential for the evolutionary stuff!

Chaos destructs ,

While order constructs,

And the puzzle how to operate them

Is in God's KNOWING STEM!

We delve into the depth of knowledge

And keep it in the mind's storage.

Every compartment of it

Is just a tiny bit

Of the universal puzzle, still intact

That we need to unravel with God in tact!

Every knowing ends up in blowing

The ignorant beliefs and IFS!

But the vastness of Universal Intelligence

Is limited by our laziness

" Know that I know nothing; the rest don't know even that."

These are the words of our ancient dad.

Socrates knew the limits of a human's grasp,

And he warned us, thus!

So, stay tuned to the new knowledge vibrations

And intelligence re-formations

In which order empowers chaos to help us defeat

The ignorance aggressive outfit!

\- - - - - - - - - - - - - - - - - - -

The direction toward mind-order:

Pseudo-attention ⟶ **Aware attention** ⟶ **Super attention!**

Holistically re-form your twisted reality de-form!

Use technology to systematize the work on Self-Ecology!

To Be Life-Gaining, Be More Self-Taming!"

(See the book " Self-Taming! in the holistic paradigm of Self-Resurrection)

"Dissipated Consciousness is a Wasted Life." *(Carl Yung)*

2. Brain has Stopped to be "Terra Incognita."

We are living at the amazing times when we are probing the new layers of life and are learning to decipher its universal text! *The material essence of thought* is being proven, *telepathy* *(transition and perception of thought at a distance)*, *parapsychology*, *(reading of thought at a distance)*, *artificial intelligence* *(the effect of Singularity)* are all being put to action. Our responsibility is to holistically put ourselves together and join the process of the natural fractal formation of everything around us.

The Fractals of Intellectually Spiritualized Beings:

Form + Content

(Body+ Spirit+ Mind) + (Self-Consciousness + Universal Consciousness)

Living Intelligence + *Enlightened Self-Consciousness = A Whole Self!*

It's gross to be negligent of the Universal Life's Force at the time of the **exponential technological growth:**

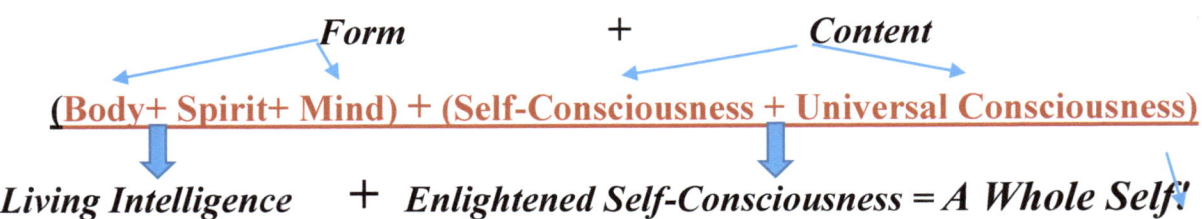

Spoken language ⟹ *written language* ⟹ *printing press* ⟹ *telephone* ⟹ *cell phone* ⟹ *the Internet* ⟹ *social media!* ⟹ *robotica* ⟹ *singularity* *and your own personal spell –*

The Self-Correcting System of the Enlightened Self!

3. Don't Be Life-Beaten!

On the cosmic plane of our life's mission,

We all fit into a certain position.

It's either life-beaten, life-smitten,

Life-paralyzed, or life-mesmerized!

Most of us

Are life–beaten by our daily fuss.

Many are life-smitten,

Some are life–paralyzed

With troubles, drugs, alcohol,

Or any other pollution device.

I belong to the last group

That survives in the life-mesmerized loop!

When life beats me, I resist,

When life twists me, I persist

In being mesmerized

With the grandeur before my eyes!

I drop my jaw

When I see a splendidly made Peugeot.

I say,"Wow!"

To the Shuttle's every space bow!

I marvel at the Internet

That is God-Set

And that unites us as One

In the Web Wide clan!

Then we can appreciate our humanness

And delete our animal-ness!

Thus, when you are life-beaten,

Or emotionally smitten,

Take a minute to think

That you need a life-wonder drink!

Open your mouth and breathe in

The prana that cleanses your inner sin.

It will help you get back

On the life-mesmerized track!

It will make you a beauty fan,

And it'll prolong your life span!

It will make you say

Without any further delay,

Long Live the Beat of "So Be It!"

4. We Are of the Five-Fold Bind

We are of a five–fold bind -

Body, Spirit, Mind, Self-Consciousness, and the Super-Mind!

They are all in a tight twine

With our evolutionary space and time!

The soul resides in the future,

 The body comes from the past,

The spirit and the mind

Are in the Now, thus!

The five ingredients of the soul -
Body, Spirit, Mind,   Self-Consciousness, and the Universal Goal.

Establish the unity with the Sun, the Earth, the water, and the air

To be in balance with life everywhere!

Intervene with *Space , Earth, Air,   Water, and Fire -.*

That's what they all define!

Which is the Dimension of Thine?

5. Don't Live in the Simulated Reality of Self-Vanity!

Be a Stoic,

Not for fun,

Get through life

<u>With an Uplifted Thumb!</u>

Don't spend your life on the political strife;

Manage it yourself for your inner politics' surf!

The Five Forces of Life: <u>Space, Fire, Air, Water, and Earth</u> determine Your Present Life's Worth!

The Structure of the Book in its Self-Inductive Nook

(The universal, spiritual, mental ,emotional, and physical

realms of life in the philosophical might.)

The Steps of Our Spiritual Infinity

(The Grains of Me and My Philosophy)

From the Commodity Capitalism to a Digitized Humanism!

Be One of a Kind in Your Body, Spirit, and the Mind!

The Steps of the Holistic Paradigm of Yours and Mine!

From the perception of the Digital Reality to the Absolute Reality without Self-Vanity!

I Try to Transmit "the Wisdom of 369" *(Nikola Tesla)* **and Make it Rhyme!**

1. Self-Perfection is the Way to Self-Resurrection!

The Matrix of a Personality Formation:

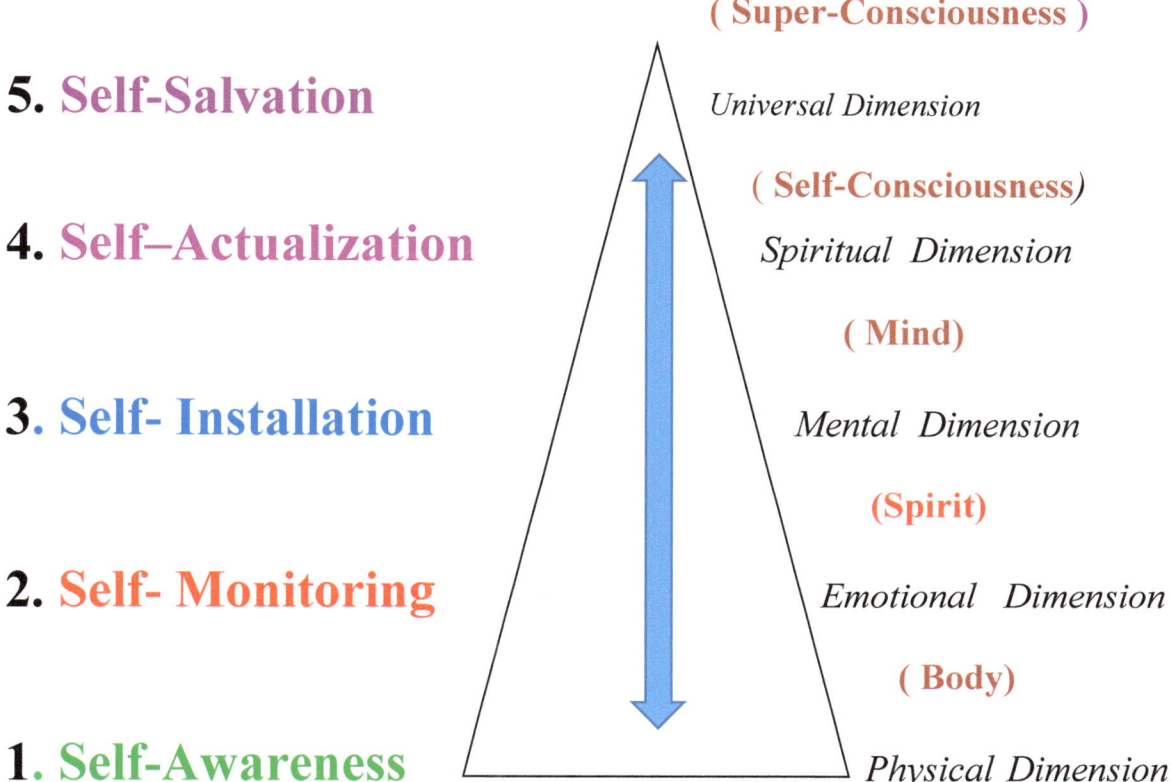

5. Self-Salvation   (Super-Consciousness)
Universal Dimension

4. Self–Actualization   (Self-Consciousness)
Spiritual Dimension

(Mind)

3. Self- Installation   *Mental Dimension*

(Spirit)

2. Self- Monitoring   *Emotional Dimension*

(Body)

1. Self-Awareness   *Physical Dimension*

The Spiritual Fractals of Being = A Soul-Refined Self!

Body + Spirit + Mind + Self-Consciousness + Universal Consciousness =

I have pinpointed here the way of performing self-change and self-growth, not as a dictator, but as an instructor who had verified this way with hundreds of students that got self-inspired and self-transformed with this vision installed. ***Visualize this route to sustain it in any mood!*** *(For more on the holistic Self-Resurrection , see* www.language-fitness.com *– **Link to video is in the section Self-Resurrection**)*

To Be Life-Inspired, you need to Get Holistically Wired!

2. Self-Salvation is in Our Spiritual Maturation!

The Process of the Spiritual Evolution is each one's life's solution! New knowledge revolutionizes our perception of the reality , making us resist, reject, and reform our old knowledge of life and living. We realize that the more we know, the less we understand, and that's our evolutionary stand!

The digital reality makes us realize that our global connection is going beyond the terrestrial boundaries , and that we need to learn to connect to the vastness of the Universal Intelligence. New knowledge helps develop new skills and new Life Awareness and Self-Awareness.

Developing our intelligence, emotional control, and willpower, we are raising our ***physical, emotional, mental, spiritual ,and universal*** awareness and shaping your self-consciousness.

" It's vital to take care of becoming better than you were before. The man who is conscious of getting better will live his life not only in the right, but also in a pleasant way." (Socrates)

So, don't focus on what you are; focus on what you can be!

The Path of Spiritual Maturation-

(Body+ Spirit+ Mind) + (Self-Consciousness + Universal Consciousness) =

A Whole Intellectually Spiritualized You!

To Life-Surf with Worth, Manage Civilly Your Life from Birth!

3. Self-Growth is Multi-Dimensional!

The five books, presented below are based on the holistic **Auto-Suggestive Psychology for Self-Ecology** in five philosophical dimensions: *physical, emotional, spiritual, mental, and universal.* The concept of process is fundamental in life.

The Holistic Pyramid of Self-Resurrection:

The Levels of Self-Resurrection: / Stages: of Self-Growth   / Books, featuring them:

5. *Universal* - *Super*-Consciousness.	**Self-Salvation**	**"Beyond the Terrestrial!"**
4 *Spiritual* - *Self-Consciousness*	**Self-Realization**	*"Self-Taming!"*
3. *Mental* - *Mind*	**Self-Installation**	*" Living Intelligence…"*
2 *Emotional* - *Spirit*	**Self-Monitoring**	*" Soul-Refining!"*
1. *Physical* - *Body*	**Self-Awareness**	*"I Am Free to Be the Best…*

<u>There's No System without the Structure!</u>

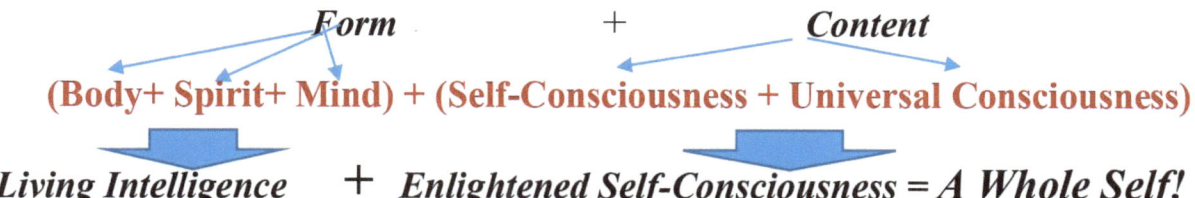

<u>*The Fractals of Spiritualized Beings:*</u>

Form + *Content*

(Body+ Spirit+ Mind) + (Self-Consciousness + Universal Consciousness)

Living Intelligence + *Enlightened Self-Consciousness = A Whole Self!*

  = *A Complete Individual or a Spiritually Refined Fractal of you!)*

All five books are illustrated with pictures and backed up with inspirational boosters. ***You can upload them to their smart phone*** in the same five levels to organize the inspirational self-boosting into the file <u>**Self-Help Hypnosis**</u> at hand.

Follow the Holistic Paradigm to help your Life's <u>Form + Content</u> Rhyme!

Life's Elation is in the Fractal Formation

Body + Spirit+ Mind + Self-Consciousness + Super-Consciousness

= A Self-Refined Fractal of you!

Our Spiritual Elation is in the Fractal Re-Formation!

4. The Self-Actualization Paradigm!

In sum, for years of my college teaching, I have had the chance to watch he change of mentality and attitude to life in the generations of students from different countries of the world.

There are numerous self-help books on the market, but the number of frustrated hearts is not lessening. We are now mastering all kinds of meditation techniques that help a lot to balance inside, but the general **KNOW-HOW** of such practices is still beyond the public at large. Admittedly, people do a lot of self-refining, but they can do it much better if they have a clear-cut plan of action in the head

Self-Awareness ⟹ Self- Monitoring ⟹ Self-Installation ⟹ Self-Realization . ⟹ Self-Salvation!

In my five books on **Self-Resurrection** *(See above),* I suggest following the **SELF-ACTUALIZATION** paradigm in **the *physical, emotional, mental, spiritual, and universal realms*** of life. I do the same in this book ,too, only with the help of the inspirational boosters and mind-sets. ***The book is structured from the top to bottom of the holistic paradigm*** because inspiration comes from the above and forms our inner stuff!

"As is Above, so it is below!"

(The Hermetic Standpoint - As it is in the head, so it is in the behavior of a person)

Step Five– **"A New Paradigm of Yours and Mine!"** *(The Universal dimension)*

At this highest level of life creation - **Self-Salvation,** *we* are supposed to acquire the ability *to live in unison with the whole of life in the Universe.* We learn to respect life in its every form become self-sufficient and wise enough to enjoy silence , balance ,and tranquility and *go beyond the terrestrial boundarie*s in our creation. **That's our inspirational start!**

Step Four – "God is Omnipresent!" (*Spiritual dimension*)

The value of life and its sacredness are based on ***the intellectualized spirituality*** and conscious following of the messages of the spiritual leaders of the past, ***self-taming*** of the bad habits that screen the grace of life. It's the level of **Self-Realization** in life formation. Happiness becomes an innate feeling of life- creation and life -elation.

Step Three –" The Odyssey of the Intellectual Aristocracy" *(Mental dimension)*;

It's the level of **Self-Installation** in life professionally and personally. You are what you think, and you think what you are! At this level, we obtain the ability to process the mind and observe the depth of self-awareness , thus ***forming our own Know-How of living.***

Step Two – "The Human Sea of the Emotional Diplomacy *(Emotional dimension);*

It's a very important level of **Self-Monitoring** in life when we are developing the ability ***to monitor our emotions and manage our feelings*** in sync with the mind. We are developing the conscious attitude to life, without speeding it up with money-raising and fun chasing.

Step One – Look at Life with the Wonder Glee and Just Be! *(Physical dimension).*

It's the level of **Self-Awareness** or the initial step for Self-Creation, when the mechanism of life is speeding up and it needs to be studied and perceived consciously to be able ***to know oneself better and to find the way to realize one's full potential,*** without destructing it in an elusive perception of the endlessness of life.

Below , all these steps are presented in the inspirationally rhyming flow.

Life's Solution is in Following the Know-How of Self-Evolution!

5. Life Must Be a Consciously Monitored Process!

To refresh your life's self-function in a nutshell, you are invited to go through the Holistic- *Universal (Step One), Spiritual (Step Two), Mental (Step Three), Emotional (Step Four),* and *Physical Level (Step Five)* of the inspirational self-boosting and self-refining in action. Beyond the five levels of self-creation , this book presents each aspect of the holistic human fractal, procuring that **the spirit should be manifested through one's own brain. Intelligence determines our life beyond survive!**

So, the inductive value of the book is in the attempt to establish the essential **HEART + MIND** unity with the help of inspirational boosters, starting **from the top to bottom** of **the Holistic Pyramid of Self-Resurrection** *(universal, spiritual, mental, emotional, and physical levels consequentially.)* **Guided by the Universal Intelligence**, we go through self-refining together with self-inspiring in a holistic unity!

Inspirational Psychology for Self-Ecology:

Step Five – **A Top Life Paradigm of Yours and Mine** - Self-Salvation Stage

Step Four - **God is Omnipresent!** – Self-Realization Stage

Step Three –**The Odyssey of the Intellectual Aristocracy** - Self-Installation

Step Two - **The Human Sea of the Emotional Diplomacy**- Self-Monitoring

Step One – **Look at Life with the Wonder Glee and Just Be!** – Self-Awareness

To Be Self-Inspired, Be Self-Redefined!

(End of the Introductory Part of the book—the Holistic Paradigm follows)

Step Five

(The Universal Uplift - Self-Salvation)

The Top Life's

Paradigm

Of Yours and

Mine!

"Every Soul Contains the Universe!"

(Feodor Dostoevsky)

I'm an Upward Leading Universal Being!

Remove the Technological Spell –

Don't Be an Alien to Yourself!

Strategize Your Thinking to Actualize the Mind + Heart Linking!

Developing your **intellectualized spirituality**, you are raising your *physical, emotional, mental, spiritual ,and universal awareness*, being channeled by the Universal Intelligence that is Above, around you, and in your every cell, *guarding you to life-excel!*

Step 5 - Be Universally Fit!

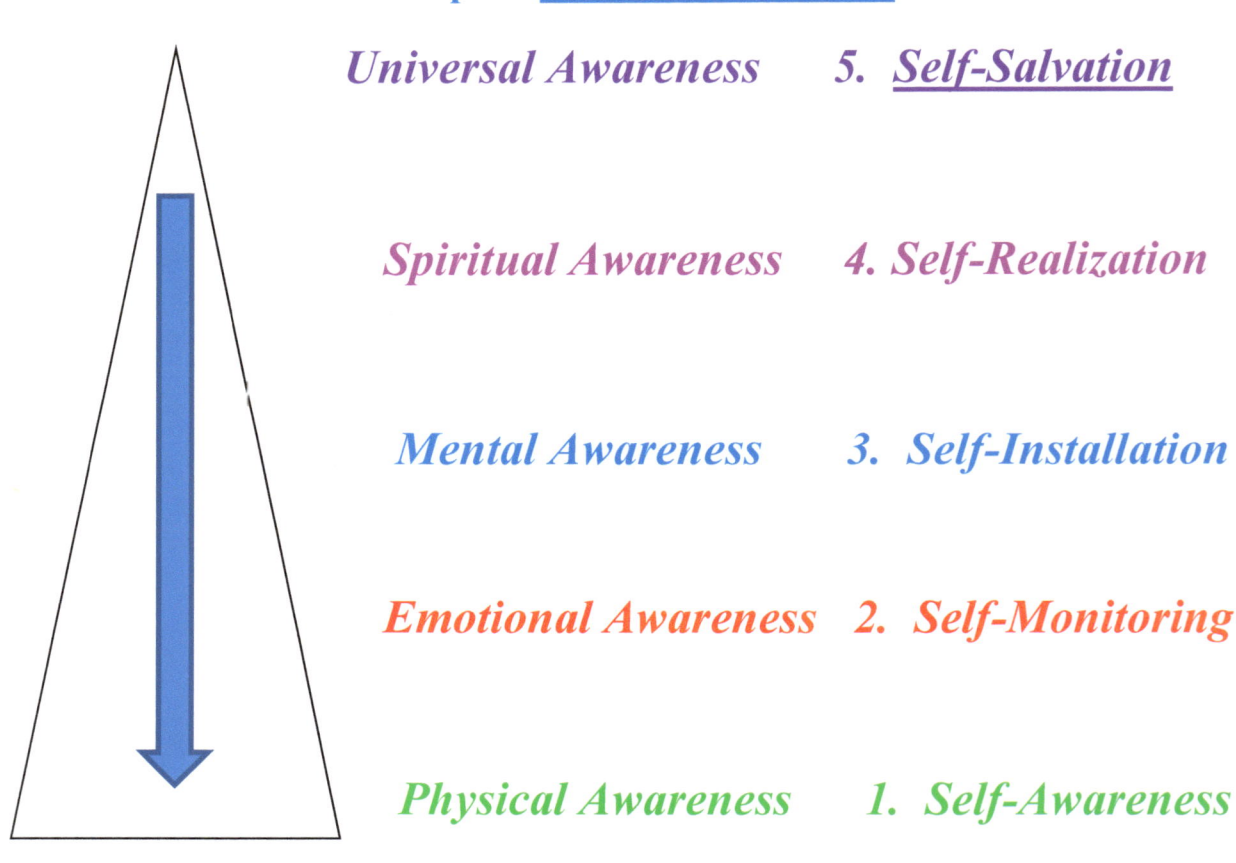

Universal Awareness   5. *Self-Salvation*

Spiritual Awareness   4. *Self-Realization*

Mental Awareness   3. *Self-Installation*

Emotional Awareness   2. *Self-Monitoring*

Physical Awareness   1. *Self-Awareness*

To be good, visualize the Self-Ecology route!

No one is perfect at large, but the reference point as such remains unchanged and untouched!

In the Universal Life Stance,

We Live but Once!

Section One

(Step Five – <u>The Universal Uplift</u> - Self-Salvation)

"*As It is Above, So, It Is Below!*" *That's Our Life's Flow!*

Use technology for Self-Ecology!

(Upload your smart phone with a new universal tone!)

As it is in Your Head, so it's in Your Mouth, Body, and the Bed!

Go Irreversibly Ahead!

1. Our Universal Constitution

We need to hit a common goal

Of the surgery of a human soul!

For our souls are full of vanity,

Pride, egotism, and profanity!

They are rotting in the love for gold

And in the chase for its every mold.

The essential truth of self-worth

Gets drowned in the deeds of human moths

Everyone is in his eggshell,

Trying hard to excel

In seeking a much easier path,

But ending up on his/ her psyche- crippled ass.

Godless self-efficacy and fake intellectualism

Build up the philosophy of internal barbarism!

The concerns of the gut

Have become an overwhelming fact!

Judging others and not knowing thyself

Is rooted deeply in every human cell.

So, let's wake up and transform

Our common material uniform

From an animal personality

To a Stellar Man's individuality!

Let's reform

Our reptilian de-form

And make the human evolution

Based on the Mutually Humaine Constitution!

- - - - - - - - - - - - - -

May the World Diplomacy reflect   the Intellectualized

Spiritual Supremacy!

(Upload your smart phone with a new inspirational tone!)

Let's not drown in the Vanity of Our Past Mentality! Let's stop looking back!

We're on the Universal Track!

2. "As It is Above, so, it is Below!"

(The Hermetic Motto)

Try to live spiritually,

And not take your problem virtually

For, "As it is Above,

<u>*So, it is below!"*</u>

That's what we should go

When we feel blue or low!

I am strong in my above ways,

<u>*But I am weak in my personal surveys.*</u>

So now, when life goes off the normal tract,

I don't declare this negative fact.

I try to ignore it and disregard,

<u>*I am quite good at that!*</u>

I am happy, anyway,

With every passing day!

And my new spiritual path

<u>*Has nothing to do with any depression mass*</u>

So, when asked, "Are you happy, or what?"

<u>*I give a straightforward "Yes" retort!*</u>

I am happy that I am alive,

Healthy, beautiful, and in love with life!

I am also in love with love

For everything below and Above!

Love is my life's load,

It's my spiritual code!

Thus, changing my emotional plane,

I shape myself spiritually again and again!

The inner dignity of the whole

Forms the aristocratism of my soul!

The Fractal of Intellectually Spiritualized Being:

Form   **+**   **Content**

(Body+ Spirit+ Mind) + (Self-Consciousness + Universal Consciousness)

Living Intelligence **+** *Enlightened Self-Consciousness* = *A Whole Self!*

Learn to Cultivate a Personal Mastery over Your Brain and Emotions Consciously." (Carl Yung)

3. To Go Forth, Clean Your Space on the Mother Earth!

(The Call for the Nature's Attitude Reinstall!)

Let's sing the panegyric of love words

To the Sun, The Ocean, the Wind, and the Earth!

They all contribute to the form of life

That we are destroying with the human might!

There's no consideration for the nuclear elation,

And there's much electronic junk even in the space rank!

The International Law not to litter the outer space and the Earth

Should be put in force!

We talk, we form societies, and make up plans,

But Nature continues to suffer from our sarcastic farce!

The dirt from the uncivil human zest

Is found even on the Everest!

The sacredness of Nature continues soaring

From our mindless gorging!

Common spiritual consideration

Is required for Nature's elation,

And biological schooling at large

Is needed very much!

Destruction starts with an ignorance splash,

That's driven by the monitory bash!

But the celebration of the profits

Turns into the restoration of the deficits,

And until we ban the Nature's destruction

Any environmental action is just a social function!

Nature is in love with us, it's a fact,

But we do not love it back!

So, until everyone commits to clean his / her dirt

The Nature will indignantly respond!

Fortify your Inner Fort; Get Aboard!

It's easier to be kind to the pets and help people declaratively than stop oneself from being nature- negligent, people- spiteful, action-resentful, life-offensive, and not self-reflexive!

Life-Gaining is in Self-Taming!

(Check out the book " *Self-Taming!* " -the spiritual levels of Self-resurrection)

www.language-ffitness.comm- link to video in the section Self-Resurrection

Not to Lifetime Spare, Be Universally Aware!

4. Be Conscious of Your Time and Space!

Be conscious of your time and

    Space,

As a lawyer of your life's

    Case!

        Don't waste them in any form,

        or for any reason,

        For it's a sure case

        of self- treason!

Life is a terminal

    Case

In its time and

    Space!

        So, defend your life

        With the sincerest bets

        To finally say,

        "I have no regrets!"

"Be Happy in Time and Space —the time you have and the Space you are in." (*Einstein*)

5. Our Universal Life Experience Validates...

Our life experience validates

What every sacred book rates

As the spiritual growth

Of the undeveloped human moths!

But it remains to be an enigma

And our personal stigma!

Negative emotions still drag us back

Onto an aloof drama personal track.

We are not yet spiritually transformed,

We are not even culturally formed!

But we are on our way

To New Consciousness bay

That on the Doom's day,

We are all reaching, per say.

Thus, our spiritual transformation

Remains to be in God's formation!

God makes us all international,

Not white, yellow, black, or national!

We are again becoming One

In His celestial tongue!

We may mean different things,

But the essence of our human wings

Takes us all to the God's domain

And makes us have the universal love vein!

It's only with this love that we can transform

Our spiritually imperfect uniform!

So, if you want to be Above the ground,

Keep Yourself Happy and Sound!

"Even the most dazzling light casts the shade."

(Winston Churchill)

To have Human Fairness , develop your Kindness, Intelligence, and

LIFE AWARENESS!

6. Artificial Intelligence

Artificial intelligence,

Is it the breakthrough or mental negligence?

Is it our contribution

To the human evolution?

Can a machine feel, hear, and think

As a human being at a wink?

Can we create an Electronic Being,

Able of loving, hearing, and seeing,

Far beyond our mental horizon

And the ability of memorizing

All the data seed

At the fingertips of our need?

Will such electronic gain

Be able to feel any pain,

And will it help me sustain an emotional storm

Of my human uniform?

How can a human robot of the future

Fall in love that is mutual?

Will the machine Being

Be able of dealing

> *With another unveiled human form*

> *Clad in an electronic uniform?*

I guess this new mechanical me

Will have a digital consciousness glee,

> *And with it, I will flee*

> *To a New Universe of Me!*

Has it happened already,

Or should we all be ready

> *To get rid of our emotional self-expression*

> *And become more mental in every dimension?*

"Everything in the Universe is Mental!"

(John Banes)

Self-Induction:

I'm Not at Rest,

I'm on the Universal Quest!

8. Be Just a Pool of Consciousness!

(An Inspirational Booster)

Be just a pool of consciousness

Create a paradise in you,

Accept life with its problems

And enjoy it, too!

"Be a light unto yourself,"

As Buddha said,

For only inner freedom can create

Your sunrise net!

You are your own glory,

Your grandeur, and your wonder

So, listen to a still voice within

It's your inner twin!

It tells you to be calm and not afraid

Of the insecurities that are in you innate

Life is tough and complex, true

But it is also natural and simple, too!

So, accept it as such

And cherish it very much!

But if you go astray in it,

Be sure to admit it!

A person who never does wrong, hardly ever grows,

That's how our life goes!

A good person

Puts bad behind him,

A bad person

Reverses this scheme

Lastly, be alone,

Not in the mob,

Be in a celibate state

With your own sob!

Remember tomorrow

Will never stay;

It's always today,

As the sages say!

Have the reins of it

In your hand,

Be the master

Of your life's band!

Also, be simple as nature,

Unpretentious and deep,

Let no one push you

To a bitter steep

Of self-guilt and imperfection,

Full of fear and self-reflection

Upon your faults and defects,

They are, but the "golden section" imperfects!

They come with each product of life,

For us to universally survive!

- - - - - - - - - - - - - - - - - -

"Be Conscious. Consciousness mobilizes!"

(Neale Donald Walsch)

Pseudo-Attention ➡ **Aware Attention** ➡ **Super Attention!**

Be always more than people could've observed before!

God Commands to Self,

" Know Thyself!"

9. To Be a Self-Savior, Stay in the Universal God's Favor!

To be always in the universal God's favor,

Follow the rules of the right mind's behavior!

Be nice, beautiful and beware,

That there're eyes and ears everywhere!

People listen and judge,

They see and plunge

Into word riots and fist fights

That only ignites their verbal bites

About what they believe in,

And how they should perceive

The values that do not hold

In the other people's mold.

True, our desire to change

Often does range

From our fake behavior modes

To the forged political votes!

We strive to change everyone else,

But remain unchanged ourselves!

To seek for a higher reference,

Be the etalons of excellence!

However, many of us, much perfect less,

Tend to become less and less!

Being nice, polite, and loving

Becomes the other side of bluffing!

The crux of the matter is

We don't want to revise this myth!

We should seek the true value of our human cells

In the spiritual wisdom wells!

For only through the Universal God's vision

Can we remove the walls for our inner revision!

(For more, check the book "Self-Taming".2019)

Life-Gaining is in Self-Taming!

It's Only through the Universal Eyes that we Revise Every Stereotyped Vice!

Section Two

(Step Five – <u>The Universal Uplift</u> - Self-Salvation)

The Philosophy

of the Right

and Wrong

To Stay on the Right Track, Work on

<u>Your Universally Spiritualized Life Act!</u>

Earth, Water, Air, Fire and the Space – Face Life, Face!

Work on the Rebirth of Air, Fire, Water, and Earth in Your Self-Worth!

1. The Philosophy of the Right and Wrong

The philosophy of the right and wrong

For centuries has undergone

A lot of verbal bites

And bloody religious fights

It was instilled in the man's race

With the birth of Christ's faith

It is with His holy mission on Earth

That we began our consciousness rebirth!

But we theorize and downsize

His evolutionary advice!

We pray, we light the candles,

But we remain vandals!

It's so incredibly hard

To have an integrity gut

That's intact and has a proper digestion

Of the truly god-ward suggestion

There's still a lot of skepticism

About Christ's moral ascetism.

So, what's right or

    Wrong

Hasn't undergone a substantial re-

    form!

                  Religion and

                  Science

                  Still remain in a de-

                  fiance,

And until they reconcile their

    Guts

The philosophy of the right and wrong will remain to be

Uguts! (Italian for "Nonsense")

           So, defy the gravity of a common-sense

           Thought

           And fly to the stars,

           <u>*No matter what!*</u>

Try to Live Right and Without a Sin Even though it Seems Obscene!

2. The Planetary Culture is in the World-Wide Structure!

The planetary culture

Is in the world-wide structure.

The Tree of Life is designed by God

To be at the core of our common life fort!

Climb its branches through the thick and thin,

Crouch, stretch, fall, jump, and swing.

Challenge yourself to come to the top,

Only then will you be close to God!

So, strengthen the element of faith

In your life' base!

Work on your inner site

And intellectually spiritualize your fractal of life!

Body+ Spirit+ Mind+ Self-Consciousness + Super-Consciousness

== An Enlightened Human Fractal

(For more on this subject, check the book " Beyond the Terrestrial", 2019)

You are Free to Be the Best of Thee!

Our Structural Ration is in the Nature's Fractal Formation!

The Sameness of life in its <u>Fractal Formation</u> is the source of our Elation!

(For more on this subject, check out the book "Beyond the Terrestrial", 2019)

<u>We are of the Same DNA - You, Me, and They!</u>

3. Make Your Mind Feel and the Heart Perceive!

Make your mind

Feel

And the heart per-

ceive

The power of

"IS"

In its life-revealing

Bliss!

Plug the void inside of

You

To protect   the sacredness of the

Two!

Manage your life at its every

twist

And appreciate it

AS IS!

Program Yourself on the Beat of Your Pulse without any Farce!

4. Be Mesmerized with the Sunrise!

Be mesmerized

With the sunrise,

With the sunset

And the stars net!

Be life enchanted

And mind-implanted

Into the mind-boggling haze

Of the universal life's base!

Be mesmerized with your time and space

That God has chosen for you to embrace!

Marvel at the time you live in

That's your life energy refill!

Use new technology for your Self-Ecology!

(Self-Induction for a better life - production)

Follow the Sunrise of Passion and the Sunset of Compassion!

5. Death Has Many Degrees for Human Pygmies!

Death has many degrees

For human pygmies!

But our physical destruction dioxins

Are not the last ones on the life's scenes!

Before a physical death comes a slow decline,

Arising from the obliteration of the spirit of Thine.

That is programmed by the digital mass

Into everyone's human ass!

People kill by drugging the will of others

And pitilessly exploiting many helpless mothers,

Returning evil for evil

And destroying the love of Eden!

Sanity, happiness, and peace of mind

Get slandered, insulted, and icily twined!

Progress is conceiving intelligent giants,

But it's producing spiritual whiners!

Conscience and human sensitivity

Evaporate speedily into the infinity!

A vast cerebral and cultural program

Is loaded into the muscles of boredom!

The messages of instant gratification

Are injected into the minds of a young generation!

The central computer of human species

Is designed for servicing the minority's riches!

The only possibility of a spiritual salvation

Is in the hands of a conscious nation

That can produce a godly leader, the spirit of whose

Is disentangled from the common digital moose!

When and where can we deserve the One,

Able to bring back our inner Sun,

Capable to ignite the minds

And take off our inhuman blinds?

I wish I could live then

In the unanswerable When?!

Love Life for its Momentum Wealth that Death 'll take with Your "Thank You" Breath!

Section Three

(Step Five - the Universal Uplift - Self-Salvation)

Don't Let Your Soul Repose And Decompose!

(Don't Be Life-Negligent, Be Life-Intelligent!)

Create Yourself in the Life-Web-Cell,

And Be Yourself!

Don't Let Your Soul Repose and Decompose!

Keep it from Decay. It Must be Working Tirelessly - Night and Day!

1. Dead Human Souls

Dead human souls

Are like filthy moles

That appear on the body of the Earth

Even at a child's birth!

A child is born with a living soul

Only if one parent has the spiritual bone,

If a child's innate admiration

Is not met with an irritated frustration.

If a child's perception of the God and the Sun

Becomes the family's rule of the thumb!

If the music of his or her spirit

Is not broken by the education in it!

And later the growth of the soul

Becomes his or her prime console!

Only then will our self-development in God

Get a real heart-felt reward!

Our lives will start to thrive

And we'll spiritually survive!

"Live and Let Live!" is the Motto of those

Who Climbs up the Spiritual Cliff!

2. Heaven Will Always Beat the Hell!

Heaven will always beat the hell,

Deleting the devil's evil spell

And making every living creature on Earth

Give God a heart-felt oath

To stop the chaos of a soul-destruction

That goes on in life without interruption!

These somber times will soon end

With the coming of Christ Consciousness bend!

The chaos will finally fall

Into the order- ruled human mall,

Lined up with stores of a national structure

That will never again be ruthlessly fractured

By the devil's tricks

On our inhumanly set bricks!

God's perfect homo sapience creation

Will get into a total reformation!

A personal soul's magic

Will stop being overly tragic

Human happiness in a harness

Will finally be God-processed!

        People will turn to light and love

        To live in harmony with the Above!

So, help me, Lord

To define my lot,

        To shine and to succeed,

        Bless me with the drive to do it!

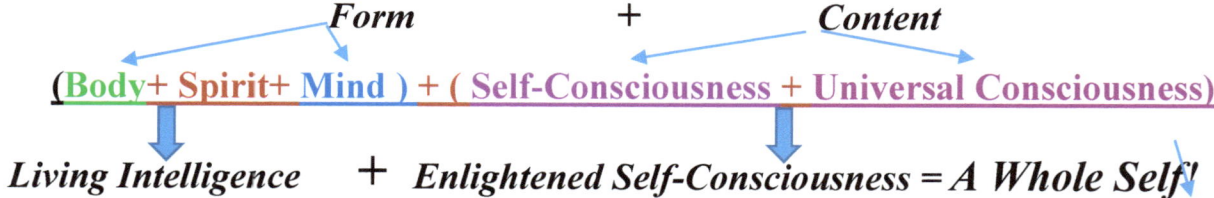

The Fractal of Intellectually Spiritualized You:

Form   +   *Content*

(Body+ Spirit+ Mind) + (Self-Consciousness + Universal Consciousness)

Living Intelligence + *Enlightened Self-Consciousness = A Whole Self!*

Tune Yourself to the Station "God,"

For Good!

3. Our Universal Unification in Love

The energies of love and light

Unite us all inside

The Universal Love seats

Is in our mutual heartbeats!

We are all One

In the God's Clan!

We are united in His Divine Love

From the below and the Above!

The God's love beat

Is also in our feet

So, as you walk,

Try to hear the God Talk

To you, to him, to Me,

"Let love be; let love be; let love be!"

Love and Light Build Up Your Energy Might!

4. Learn to Bear Each Other's Burden!

Bearing each other's burden

Is the law that is in us rotten!

Being patient even with one's own burden,

Poses already a big personal problem!

The law of immediate gratification

Produces much more elation!

But whether we like it or not,

All of us will report to God!

He'll weigh the burden that we have carried,

As well as the one that we have discarded.

Everyone's spiritual X-Ray

Will be at play!

And our Heaven or hell's array

Will be the God's final say!

So, learn the Lesson without missing

That every burden is a blessing!

Life is the Art of Seeing with

the Mind + the Heart in a Being!

5. Be Faithful to Your Soul; Fulfilled Life is its Goal!

Put the Mind and the Heart

in Sync –

Feel but Think!

Don't let Your Books die

on the shelf!

Don't Self-Shelf!!!

Use the Auto-Suggestive Meditation for Inner Consideration!

(See the Know-How Part - Section Two)

Self-Persuasion has an Incredible Power of Mind-Invasion!

Step Four

(Step Four - _The Spiritual Uplift_ - _Self-Realization_)

God is

Omni-

Present!

"Life at its Best is the Life of Faith!

(_"Dr. Stanley_)

The More God You Have Inside, the More Happiness You Get Outside!

Our Spiritual Quest Remains to Be Abreast!

On the Religiously Different Porch,
God is One on His Everlasting Watch!

Strategize Your Thinking to Actualize Your <u>Mind + Heart</u> Linking!

Step 4 (<u>Be Spiritually Fit!</u>)

Universal Awareness	**5.** <u>**Self-Salvation**</u>
Spiritual Awareness	**4.** <u>**Self-Realization**</u>
Mental Awareness	**3.** **Self-Installation**
Emotional Awareness	**2.** **Self-Monitoring**
Physical Awareness	**1.** **Self-Awareness**

<u>"Our Holiness is in Being Whole!"</u>

(Deepak Chopra)

(Upload your smart phone with a visual zone!)

Not to Lifetime Spare, Be Holistically Life Direction Aware!

Section One

*(Step Four - The Spiritual Uplift – **Self-Realization**)*

"We are too

Spiritually

Near-Sighted."

(David Icke)

"Don't Look for God in Churches!

God is inside you!" *(Leo Tolstoy)*

1. God is Omnipresent!

God is omnipresent,

He is in you, me, and the President!

God is our past, present, and the future,

He is our life that is mutual!

God is like the Sun,

He is impartial to everyone!

No religion, skin color, or a bank account

C-o-u-n-t!

On the universal ladder of the evolution

We are a homo-sapience step in motion

We were evolved to a human position,

As a God-given mission

To construct, to reason,

To love without any treason,

To help each other to survive,

To raise yourself spiritually and to thrive!

But we destroy, kill, and fight,

We often act as animals in sight!

Millions of years of our evolution

Have only increased the human pollution!

We have created wonders of digital technology,

But we remain animals in our emotional eulogy.

So, how can the Omnipresent God

Manage to stop the instinct-driven mob?

There is only one solution

For the human evolution

And that is to change our spiritual gas

And turn into the Star People, thus!

"The eyes of God are everywhere,

keeping watch on the wicked and the good."

(Proverbs 15:3)

"To Follow Your Bliss,"(Joseph Campbell)

Make a Strong Spiritual Twist!

God's Watchful Eye is Inside and Outside Your Life's Site!

Глаз природы

Our Inner Fest is in addressing God in any form without any religious de-form!

"In the Name of Allah – the Entirely Merciful, the Exceptionally Merciful." *(Koran)*

2. Religion or Spirituality - Unity or Duality?

Religion is a choice

Spirituality is your inner voice

Religion is blaming,

Spirituality is framing!

Religion is interpreting , scaring, and ignorant,

Spirituality is self-performed, liberating, and infinite!

We declare our faith in God,

But we know very little of What

Is written in the unread midst

Of the Torah, the Bible, or the Koran's sacred width

The search for the truth of the sin

Remains to be boring, hard, and obscene!

We are too life-rushed

To give the mind a thinking flash!

We swallow an interpreter's info

About what the sacred books' messages are for!

Why does the general crowd

Get stubborn and wouldn't spout

The beauty of the incredible plan

About a human life's span?

Why do we continue to dis regard

The feelings of the gut?

Our intuition is in a recession,

It's not in the God's session.

So, let's try and seek the reward

In the spiritual where and what

We have to reform

In our imperfect religious uniform!

"Religion is following the messenger;

Spirituality is following the message!

(Sadhguru)

Self-Evolution will help us Revolutionize
and Become Spiritually Wise!

3. Do Not Question the Universal God!

Do not question the Universal

   God

That's your main spiritual

   Fort!

   Just to inwardly believe

   And to be totally relieved

Of your past life

   Sin

That can never become ob-

   scene!

   Unless, of course, you are with God

   In your everyday thought!

 To be less spiritually deprived,

<u>Try to be Godly Right!</u>

(Self-Induction for a better Life Production)

<u>In My Thought, I Report Only to God!</u>

4. The Me-God Interaction

The Me-God interaction

Is full of a spiritual fraction

I often profess,

But God provides and invests

Into the Universal Plan

Of my life-watched span.

I expect, but God inspects

The evil twists of my inner beasts.

I promise, I pray,

But God listens in dismay

To the authenticity of my says

That are often lacking in faith!

When I suffer a lot, I talk to God

"Why don't you help me, Lord?

The answer comes with the frustration

Of my late inner realization

That my imploring

Is often empty and boring.

There're No Responses to My Pleas and Dismays without the Proof of My Faith!

5Faith Without Love is a Frozen Stuff!

Unfreeze Your Love Striptease!

5. I Put My Actions in Sync with God's Wink!

God is my future, present, and the past,

God is my life's mast!

He holds up both of my sails

From falling into the stormy life waves!

He teaches me to have faith

And walk on the water;

He shows me how to face

My fears at every life's quarter!

With God, I can ban and smear

Every bit of my fear!

I don't let it master me

When I am full of spiritual glee!

God fills my sails up with courage

To beat the devil's tempting bondage

With His name on my lips

I delete his many evil deeds

I win, I conquer, I empower

With His unbeatable power!

We Can do Whatever we want to Only with God in Me and You!

6. Don't Let Anybody Run Your Mind and the Body!

I don't let anybody

Run my mind or the body!

No one is in charge

Of my life that much!

"Let God and let go!"

Is the motto of my life's show!

Only the Almighty God

Can tell me What

I should or shouldn't do

 With my personal life's ado!

On the path of spiritual advancement,

I need a lot of enhancement!

In the long run,

Everyone is run

By the cycle of the evolution,

As the life's final solution!

In Your Thought, Report Only to God!

Section Two

(Step Four - the Spiritual Uplift - Self-Realization)

Praying

is

Life-Gaining!

Use your Smart Phone for the Unification Tone!

(See the Know-How Part - Section Two)

Support Your Inner Fort with

Praying to God!

1. I Keep Saying in My Praying

(An Inspirational Prayer)

I keep saying Christ's words

In my praying:

"I am the salt of the Earth,

I am the light of the world,

I'm the city on the hill… "

I am free to feel the God's Free Will!

I do not judge,

Nor do I ever plunge

Into swearing, cursing, resisting, or

An evil person's fisting.

I even practice loving the enemy

For my inner godly harmony

That keeps the bad and the good

Under the God's hood.

Trying to be perfect like that

Is exceedingly hard!

But who said that believing is easy,

Is that you, or a stupid Lezzy?

So, take life as it comes

And let God bless its outcomes!

Be a good humankind,

The One with the Universal Mind!

Take yourself more seriously

And work on your soul religiously!

Sustain the test of your life's quest

With a Strong Spiritual zest!

And don't ever fall into a depression oblivion,

Life is always worth your living on and on!

With the Grace of God,

I'm living On-ward, For-ward, and Up-ward!

What is your direction toward!

Auto-Induction:

I Never Lose the Sight of

My Divine Might!

2. God, How Much Should I Take?

God, how much should I take?

What is the limit of my intake?

> *When will You banish*
>
> *My being punished*

For my naiveté and sincerity,

For the lack of wisdom and dexterity,

> *For my stupidity*
>
> *In its bare nudity,*

And for my disgrace

For the lack of faith?

> *Why am so severely judged*
>
> *And hardly ever obliged*

With a little bit of luck

That is not fucked.

> *Why is my goodness never rewarded,*
>
> *Why does evil, unpunished, fault it?*

What is your logic,

Or is it forged?

Does one have to believe in God,

Without expecting any reward?

So, what comes forth

In the spiritual growth?

Who will give me the retort,

The devil or God?

Here, I hear the Say

From the Above array,

"Whenever you feel blue or mentally distraught,

Start entertaining the constructive thought

That only your body, spirit, and mind in unity

Will build up your anti-evil immunity!"

"Let me see, and I would believe.

First, believe, then you'd see!"

Long Live the Belief in God

Without "If"!

3. At Every Life's Curve

At every life's curve,

We should worship and serve "the Lord, Our God!"

"Fishers of men", we could be made,

If we followed what God bade!

Then we will be worthy

Of His unbelievable mercy!

For only if we are blessed and blessing

Do we get His precious professing!

Only then can the purity of His spirit and heart

Become the care of a human gut!

We are also blessed if we are "Meek,

Merciful and peace-making in our seek"

Finally, we need "to rejoice

In our inner voice"

And be "exceedingly glad"

"For great is the reward in heaven for that!"

Only then do inner demons get aghast and leave you free

With Christ's Consciousness rooted in Thee!

"Inga Nature Renovator Integrate!"

4. In My Thought, I Report Only to God!

Christ said under the disciples' hungry watch,

"On this rock, I will build my Church!"

And so, I do,

Building my church inside myself and you!

For the rock of your self-worth

Is here, on Earth

And your church will sit

On the top of it!

Your thoughts and feelings

Make up your congregation dealings

You are the formation

Of your own obligation!

But your church exists and prospers

Only on the bricks of the sacred Gospels!

So, visit your inner church as often as you can

To prolong your spiritual life span

And commit to God on the porch

Of your personally built church!

Remember, Some Day is Today!

To Balance Yourself,

You Need to Program Your Cells!

Use the Auto-Suggestive Meditation for Inner Unification!

(See the Know-How part - Section Two)

We are Still Very Young in the Evolutionary Plan!

5. *"Say a Prayer before You Step forward into the Day" without any Dismay!* (Edgar Cayce)

"Here I am, Oh God!

Use me, send me, as Thou sees.

Not my will, but Thine!

Oh God! Be done in and

through me.". (Edgar Cayce)

- - - - - - - - - - - - - - - - -

God is at my Right Side.

Christ (Allah, Buddha, Krishna etc) *is at my Left Side!*

Light is Inside!

Light is My Might!

Paying is Life-Sustaining!

6. Praying is Also Self-Sustaining!

Auto-Induction:

Today is a New Day

In Every Way!

I Think, Speak, and Act

With God in a Spiritual tact!

I'm a New Me -

I'm as good as

I could Ever Be!

Halleluiah to a New Day in Me!

Mobilize, Don't Immobilize Your Spirit and its Inner Size!

Step Three

(Mind-Sets against Mental Inertia - Self-Installation)

The Odyssey
of the Intellectual
Aristocracy

(For more on the mental dimension, see the Excellence Award winning book / March 2020 - "Living Intelligence or the Art of Becoming!"

"Focus on Your Mental Needs, not Emotional Wants!" (Antony Robins)

Consciousness is Everywhere and in Everything!

(Even in a Rock Seeing , there is a Thinking Being!)

People don't have Bad Brains; they just have Bad Programs in their Brains" *(Laureli Blyth)*

Strategize Your Thinking to Actualize Your Mind + Heart Linking!

Step 3 (Be-Mentally Fit!)

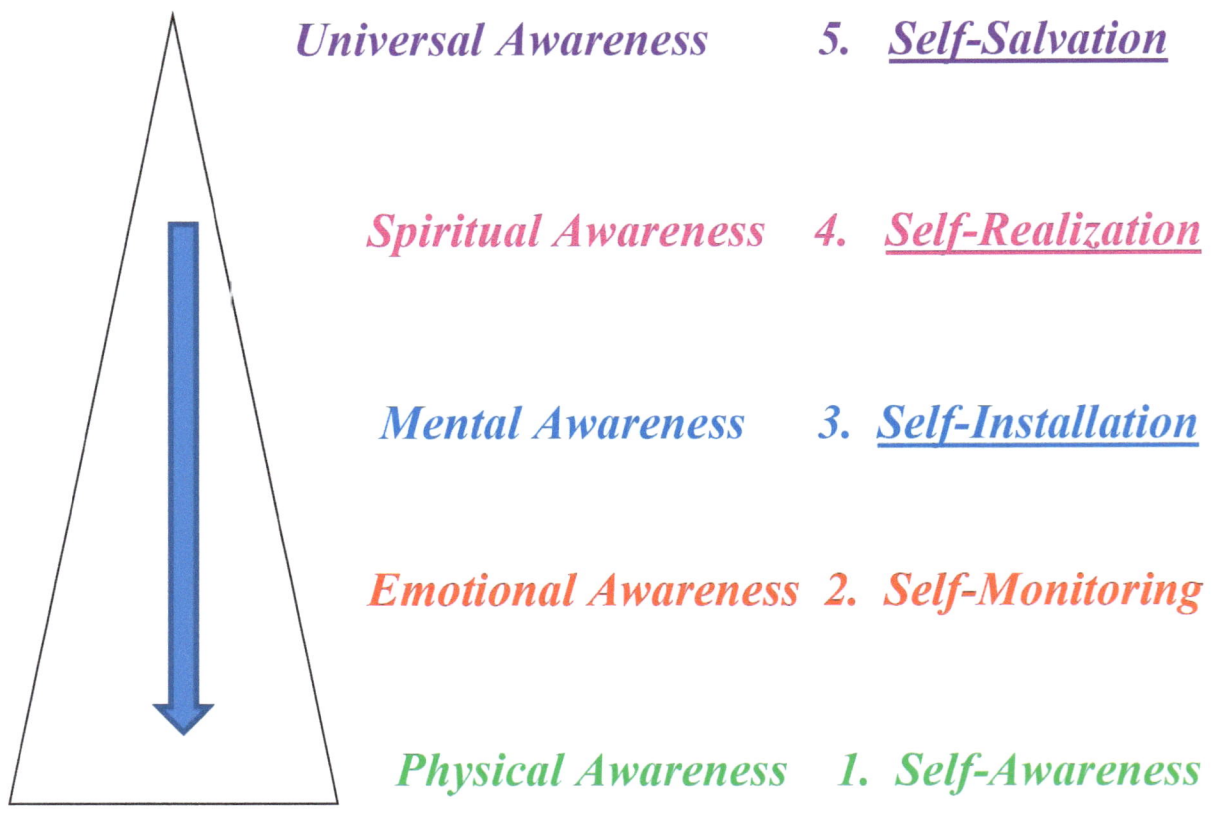

Universal Awareness   5.   Self-Salvation

Spiritual Awareness   4.   Self-Realization

Mental Awareness   3.   Self-Installation

Emotional Awareness 2. Self-Monitoring

Physical Awareness   1. Self-Awareness

Intelligence is the Feeling of Wholeness!

"The best way to self-improvement is by perfecting your thoughts!"
Leo Tolstoy

Not to Lifetime Spare, Be Holistically Life Direction Aware!

Section One

*(Step Three - Mind-Sets against Mental Inertia - **Self-Installation**)*

Every New Technological Snap makes us change Our Cognitive Map!

Pseudo Attention ➡ **Aware Attention** ➡ **Super Attention!**

1. Information ➡ Transformation

Physical, emotional, mental, spiritual, universal vistas of

Intelligence to be installed:

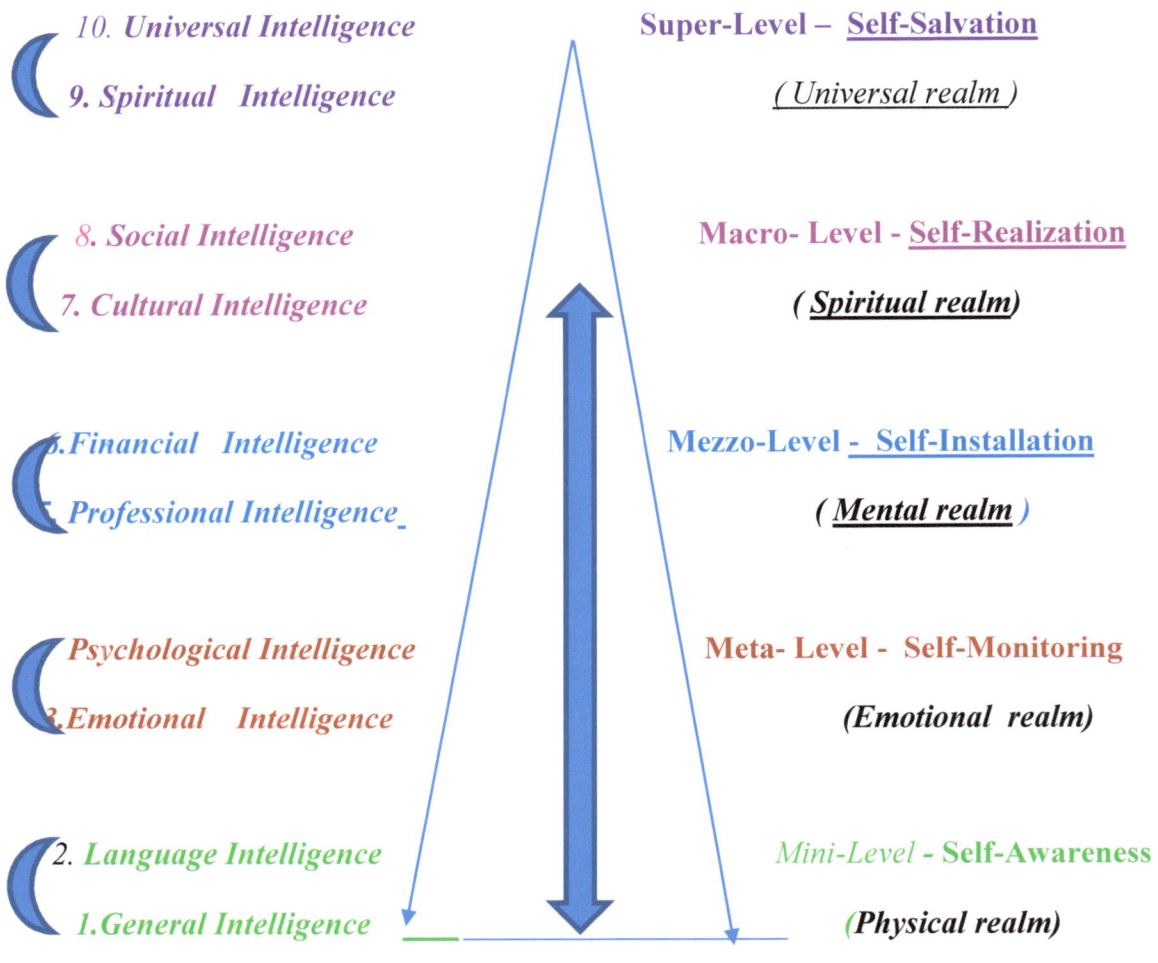

10. Universal Intelligence	Super-Level – Self-Salvation
9. Spiritual Intelligence	(Universal realm)
8. Social Intelligence	Macro- Level - Self-Realization
7. Cultural Intelligence	(Spiritual realm)
6.Financial Intelligence	Mezzo-Level - Self-Installation
Professional Intelligence	(Mental realm)
Psychological Intelligence	Meta- Level - Self-Monitoring
Emotional Intelligence	(Emotional realm)
2. Language Intelligence	Mini-Level - Self-Awareness
1.General Intelligence	(Physical realm)

/ Physical / Cognitive / Digital

New *Educational Awareness* presupposes a **_new holistic, technologically enhanced outlook,_** based on the knowledge of each vista of intelligence at least at the dilettante level...

"It's Not Enough to Be the Best;

Be the Only!" (Steve Jobs)

2. _WOW!_ _I Live NOW!_

My goal in life

is to prove

my exceptional

techno-personal might!

Use Technology for Your Self-Ecology!

(Upload your smart phone with a new educational tone!)

Stay on the Track of Signing the Technologically Advanced Self-Pact!

3. I Can…! I Want to…! And I Will…!

Visualize the pyramid of the *Vistas of Intelligence* (*See Ch. 1 above*) and **keep it at the forefront of your mind**. Monitor your breathing while programming the inductions in every intelligence. Below, there is an example how to do it, using *the* main ACTUANABLE MIND-SET.

I can ⟹ (*breathe in*) I want to ⟹ *(Pause)* and I will ⟹ (Breathe out)

The Vistas of Intelligence to install with this self-induction:

1. *Physical Intelligence* - **I can be** *healthy, radiant, happy, and content!* **(I want to…, and I will …!)**
2. *Language Intelligence* – **I can control** *my tongue!* **(I want to… and I will** *be in control of my language.)*
3. *Emotional Intelligence* - **I can be** *emotionally diplomatic, disciplined, and balanced.* **(I want to… and I will …!)**
4. *Psychological Intelligence* - **I can be** *self-confident, unbeatable, and self-reliant.* **(I want to… and I will …!)**
5. *Professional Intelligence* – **I can be** *professional, knowledgeable, creative, and very successful.* **(I want to…, and I will …!)**
6. *Financial Intelligence* – **I can be** *financially-intelligent, money-disciplined, and monetary-secure.* **(I want to…and I will …!)**
7. *Cultural Intelligence* - **I can be** *considerate, respectful, and culturally mindful* **(I want to…, and I will …!)**
8. *Social Intelligence* – **I can be** *sociable, friendly, and very cooperative.* **(I want to…, and I will …!)**
9. *Spiritual Intelligence* – **I can be** *faithful, loving, kind, and giving.* **(I want to…, and I will…!)**
10. *Universal Intelligence* – **I can be** *a real luminary, spiritually - connected, life-aware, and soul-shiny!* **(I want to…, and I will …!**

(*For more, check the Excellence Award Winner,2020 - "**Living Intelligence or the Art of Becoming!**"- the mental level of Self-Resurrection)*

A More Informed Being has a Better Professional Seeing!

4."Be Conscious; Consciousness Mobilizes"

(Neale Donald Walsch)

Consciously refine your

physical, emotional, mental, spiritual and universal spine!

(Body+ Spirit+ Mind) + (Self-Consciousness + Universal Consciousness) =

The paradigm of your mental life to consciously survive:

Synthesis - Analysis - Synthesis!

Generalize – Select - Internalize - Strategize -Actualize!

Follow this holistic business rule!

*(For more, see the book "" **I'm Free to be the Best of Me**!- the initial physical level of self-resurrection. / www.language-fitness. com. / the link to the video is in the section Self-Resurrection)*

Follow the route of Mental Modification without frustration!

Self-Awareness  **Self- Monitoring** ➡ **Self- Installation** ➡ **Self-Realization** . ➡ **Self-Salvation**

Learn to Operate Holistically Your Mind's Device and Be Overly Wise!

5. Intellectual Aristocracy

I belong to a rare class,

Found in every human mass

It's an intellectual aristocracy

That has the power of mental obstinacy!

We hit the ignorance at large,

For it holds the world in grips so much!

But the intellect of a few

Is still very brittle in view,

And the ignorance of so many

Is at the battle for a penny!

Intelligence goes by very subtle ways

For it to truly surface!

The aristocracy of the mind

Still must unwind

The hidden midst

Of its inner width

In each and every one,

Fed up with the infinite fun!

We are supposed to seek a narrow way

For a spiritual survey!

We fill up our digital mind

With the life cells ready to rewind

The double helix of an animal DNA

Into a four-dimensional Star Man's display!

But now with Steve Jobs being away,

Who in charge of our intellectual bay?

Being just smart doesn't form your spiritual gut!

Systematize ➡ **Analyze** ➡ **Strategize!**

Knowing something is indispensable, knowing everything is impossible, *knowing more is IRRIVERSIBLE!*

Let's Unite as One Cell in a Vast Universal Spell!

6. You Are What You Think!

You are what you think,

And you think what you are.

       That is the God's

       Mental formula!

Your intellectual form

Shapes your physical uniform!

       It also reforms

       Your emotional forms

You develop as a human being

With a broader vision of seeing!

       You build up your personality,

       Devoid of a selfish vanity

Deep thinking

Is like drinking!

       It intoxicates

       The mind-body debates!

And it changes the face

Of your personal interface

The mind is monitoring the brain again!

So, think broader,

Breathe deeper,

And always self-emote

With your thinking remote!

Make your body and mind stand in line

In the space-time twine

Thus, you'll join the club

Of the transformed thinkers' rehab!

In My Thought, I'm the Elite of the World!

"If you want to go fast, go alone,

but if you want to go far, go together!"

(Steve Jobs)

The Quality of Your Life is the Quality of Your Thoughts!

Section Two

(Step Three -   Mind-Sets against Mental Inertia - Self-Installation)

"Life is the Test of Patience when you have nothing , and the Test of Behavior when you have everything!" *(Jack Ma)*

Don't Enrich the Hell in your Inner Shell!

"Ignorance is the worst enemy of the humanity." (Albert Einstein)

Adversity Reveals; Prosperity - Conceals!

Consciousness is the Universal Language of Life!

"I Think, Therefore I Am!"

(Descartes)

1. Intelligence or Ego?

Like every intelligent person, I have a dilemma

How to separate my intelligence from the Ego problemma?

Intelligence is colorful and light,

While ego is colorless and uptight!

It ignites the minds that are dark

With the mob psyche's spark!

Intelligence is a privilege and a glory;

Ego is an agony, and a selfish folly!

Intelligence is an open sky

With it, we can all fly!

With it, you are not an individual snob,

And you are not a part of the mob!

With the Ego, in reverse,

You are on a lost course!

You drug, or drink,

And you need to see a shrink!

Ego is also stupid,

While intelligence is lucid!

Where there's harmony, there's strength and intelligence,

But where there's an Ego, there's weakness and negligence!

One should remain a living process,

One should never become at thing!

Like a person, taking drugs, we should admit

Is becoming exactly a dehumanized "It!"

He might go up the fame ladder of the Hollywood Hill,

But he'll end up downward any time still

- - - - - - - - - - - - - - - - - - -

So, the choice is yours

And if you are not a human moth,

Only intelligence will reverse

Your lost life's course!

- - - - - - - - - - - - - - -

To Be Emotionally Strong and Mind-Smart.

Establish Connection between the Mind and the Heart!

Learn the Art of Mindful Thinking!

2. Creativity and Imagination

Creativity and imagination

Intuition and cooperation

Logic and inner steel

Make you strong and still!

I try to be proactive,

Not reactive

I try to drive my mental mobile and rein

Over the life's emotional terrain

I practice my spirit's reformation

With the help of an everyday elation.

I generate the paradigm

That is exceptionally mine!

Inspiration or desperation

That's the equation of my elation!

Thus, with God in sync,

I am what I think!

Be Smart, but Don't Let Down Your Noble Guard!

3. Your Head Creates Your World!

Your head creates your world

Only when you are looking forward!

When you widen your mind

And uplift your spirit,

When you are ready to unwind

The best of you in it!

When you hurry to do good

And always stay in a great mood,

When your inner uniqueness

Outshines your outer bleakness,

When a Big You

Is ready to stand up for the Two -

For yourself out there

And for that guy somewhere!

When your voice is heard, too

And is often referred to, as a guru

When you get the Sun

Out of your inner pocket.

Each morning that you step

On the life's docket!

When the others' emotional space

Is given respect to surface,

When a small you is enslaved

By the willpower that you've always craved,

When the mental and emotional You

Come in lieu for a full view.

Only then will the unity of the two

Start building up a New You!

P.S. I sometimes hear from my students, " I like your theory very much, but I have no money *"to actualize myself."*

When there's no money base, there' s no time for Self-Space!

That's very rue. Here's what **Socrates** said to one of his pupils to the same complaint in response to his request to give him advice where to get the money to develop himself the way he instructed them.

" Borrow money from yourself! When the student exclaimed in surprise , "How?" Socrates replied, " Decrease your wants and learn to be content with the essential needs. Then, you'll live in a sufficient space for Self-Grace!"

"For as a Man Thinks in His Heart, so is He!" (Proverbs, 23:7)

4. I'm an Egghead!

I live in my head,

I am an egghead!

Thinking is my Being,

It's my feeling and seeing!

All I've got

Is food for thought

I fill up my mind's storage

With very much knowledge

I process it and cleanse it from clutter

Of the redundant info-matter

So, I can have a clear head,

And I don't get mentally bereft

With any emotional residue

Of my personal life's view

I write it down in the space and time ink

To keep my head and heart in sync!!

We Need to Pay More Heed to the Richness of the Mind in the Humankind!

To Balance Yourself,

You Need to Program Your Cells!

The chaos of our past lives is directing us to the order of the present and the future that is mutual!

We are Very Young in the Evolutionary Plan!

5. Science is Mesmerizing Me!

Science is mesmerizing me

With the infinity of its glee!

As we are all evolving,

Science is revolving

Around the new secrets in stride

And about the mysteries of life

How can one be bored and depressed

When it's hard not to be obsessed

With the desire to see, to feel, and to know

All about the life's flow on the go?

Science is uplifting the mind

To the heights that help us unwind

The hidden wealth

Of our creative depth

So, let's ask questions and question our illusions

For the validity of the scientific solutions!

Let's continue to stay in awe

Of God, Life, and All!

Think as a Man of Action,

But Act as a Man of Thought!

6. Put Your Brain in Gear - Mind Steer!

Put your brain in gear,

And actively steer

>> *To knowledge and skills*

>> *In all their infinite fields!*

But don't be scared to overfill

Your personal brain's mobile!

>> *It can take tons of informational gas*

>> *That will launch you high very fast*

To success and rewards,

To new avenues and amazing thoughts

>> *To the God's domain*

>> *That is like His celestial mane*

But your every brain cell needs to be in synch

With the God's responding wink!

>> *You need to be on a mission*

>> *To His domain's admission!*

So, think in excess

How to process

The entire spiritual info

That you'd gotten before.

Only then

Will you be able to spell

The God's universal plan

For your meaningful life span!

The quality of your life is in the hands of your mind.

Start with being One of a Kind!

Developing your intelligence, you are raising your

physical, emotional, mental, spiritual , and universal awareness.

Use technology for your Self-Ecology!

Be Your Own Lawyer

with the Capital "L"- Self-Excel!

7. Food for Thought

We need a Lot

Food for Thought

> To analyze and to reflect,
>
> To consider and to project!

But our brain stomachs develop an inflammation

From the clutter of digital   information

> How do I get on a diet
>
> Of a good, sorted out mind,

The mind that can delete

The redundant info-shit,

> The mind that will store
>
> Only what I need and no more?

Are there any pills or meals

To obtain the brain of the best deals?

> Yes, I say, there is a solution
>
> For a human mind's evolution!

Discipline it and keep it clean

Before it becomes obscene!

Also, say what you mean

And mean what you say

To be totally clear

At the social bay!

But try not to smear

Your right brain's hemisphere!

Learn to systematize and to revise,

Don't permanently analyze!

Don't let your brain become a full zone

For a dirty electronic phone

Use it rationally and to the purpose

To be always in the mental focus!

Finally, do not forget to cut your talk,

Better walk, walk, and walk.

Exercise and read a lot

To have much food for thought!

Lighten up and Power up in Your Inner Rehab!

8. Manage Your Money!

Manage your money without negligence,

Acquire some financial intelligence!

Poor people are greedier than the rich,

They are much more money-bewitched

But having and doing go with them in reverse

And, therefore, there's no money in their purse!

You need to invest in your greatest asset,

It's your mind faucet!

Turn on the thinking tap,

Let the brain watering fill up your money gap

Also, learn to work with the people not below, but above you,

This way you won't blow what's due to you!

Also, develop your money management skills

To climb up great prosperity hills!

Money and confidence come in unity,

Together they build up your financial immunity!

If Financial Intelligence is Low, Money will
be Smarter than you. Be in Control of the Two!

9. Let's Remove the Money Rule!

Let's remove the money rule

And mark this century with a love boom!

Let's revive our love life

To spiritually survive!

Love is the hardest job, that's true,

But we are humans, not mildew!

Why do we keep trading love for a dollar,

Like it was in Sodom and Gomorra?

How long are we going to weigh

Love with the bank account display?

When will we start to appreciate

Every one's mind's shape,

His or her uniqueness,

The absence of bleakness,

The strength of the spirit,

And the width of a soul in it?

Only these qualities will outweigh

Any bank account display!

So, Let's Celebrate the Time to Come with Love's Booming Outcome!

10. To Mentally Survive,

Follow the Three Main Rules in Life.

(Spiritual Reminder)

"Reject - Resist - Reform"

(Rabbi Berg / "Taming the Chaos")

Your Inner De-form!

To follow God and to be happy in life, no matter what, is not just to be kind, do good things, frequent the church, and pray when life gets sour, **but it also means to** TAME YOURSELF physically, emotionally, mentally, spiritually and universally and *refrain from thinking, saying, feeling, and doing bad things to yourself and others* by transforming yourself into a much better human being who never forgets to command to himself,

(Upload your smart phone with a Self-Educational tone!)

Reject, Resist, Reform!

Put on the Intellectually Spiritualized Uniform!

11. Create a Mental Binder for the Inspirational Reminder:

Self-Induction for life -Production:

I Embrace My Life

in its Entire Mass

for it Too

Shall Pass!

Use the Auto-Suggestive Meditation for Inner Elation!

(See the Know-How Part – Section 2)

Life is Me;

Life is My Philosophy!

<u>Step Two</u>

(Inspirational Boosters and Mind-sets <u>for an Emotional Uplift</u>)

Self-Monitoring State

The Bottomless Sea

of the Emotional

<u>Diplomacy</u>

Inner Emotional Balance is the Feeling of Wholeness!

(Upload your smart phone with an Emotionally Diplomatic tone!)

To Be Able to Swim in the Human Sea, Acquire More <u>Emotional Diplomacy</u>!

Make the Hear Smart and the Mind
Kind. Be One of a Kind!

Solarize Your Soul with Intelligence,
Kindness, and Self-Control!

Strategize Your Thinking to Actualize the Mind + Heart Linking!

Step 2 -Self-Monitoring!

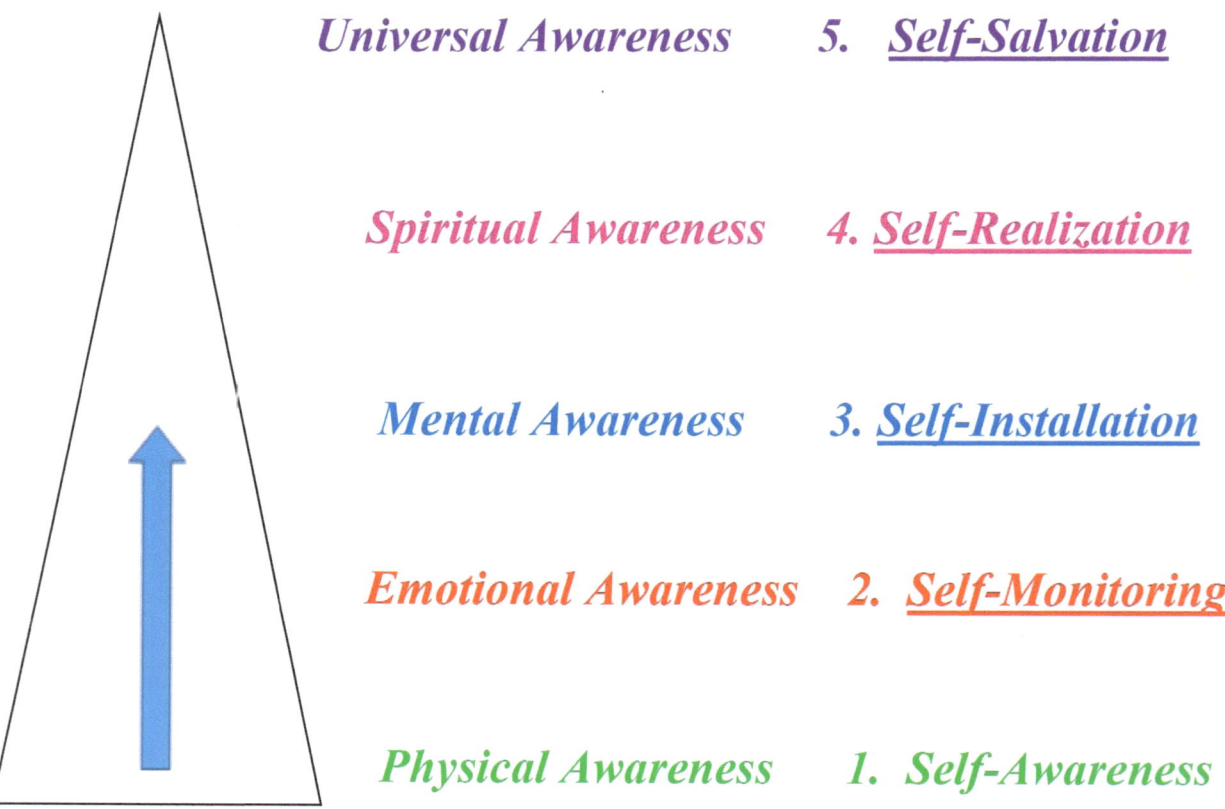

Universal Awareness   5.   Self-Salvation

Spiritual Awareness   4. Self-Realization

Mental Awareness   3. Self-Installation

Emotional Awareness   2. Self-Monitoring

Physical Awareness   1. Self-Awareness

To become Soul-Wise, activate Your Mind + Heart device!

Not to Lifetime Spare, Be Holistically Life Direction Aware!

Section One

(*Step Two* - *The Emotional Uplifts*- **Self-Monitoring**)

Stabilize

Your Emotional

Pendulum!

"A stupid person gives vent to all his feelings, but a wise one calmly keeps them in check." (*Proverbs 29, 11*)

(*For more See the book* **"Soul-Refining!"**- *Emotional dimension in the Paradigm of Self-Resurrection* -*www.language-fitness.com*)

Upload your Smart Phone with a New Emotional Tone!

1. <u>*Life-Gaining is in Self-Taming!*</u>

Being perfect is unrealistic

If not Self-Sadistic!

But it's hardly possible,

<u>*So, why not try and make your vices reversible?*</u>`

Why not stop justifying others and ourselves

<u>*And start cleansing your mental spells*</u>

That are often self-inflicted

<u>*And remain undeleted.*</u>

So, place your change waver

<u>*In charge of the God's favor!*</u>

Set the Control over Your

<u>*God-Given Soul!*</u>

2. Like Einstein

Like Einstein, I travel on the beam of

light

When I'm down and blue

inside!

I send myself up to the cosmic

space

To demagnetize my toxic mental

base!

I remove there my spiritual size

Ban,

And lengthen up my lifetime

Span!

Thus, I energize my batteries

Anew

And come back to Earth,

Like new!

Inspiration or Desperation- that's Our Life's Equation!

3. Look Life in Face in Time and Space!

Look life in face

In time and space!

Don't ever swoon

At the Sun, or at the Moon!

Confront your fears and doubts,

Don't let them shoot the sprouts

That root in your mood

And rotten up your mental food

When you look life in face,

You gain a tougher faith

In God, in yourself,

In life itself!

So, I'm repeating on and on,

"Life is beautiful, and it's going on!"

It's more than enough to make you mile

And help you once more to redefine

The life that proceeds, as it normally does,

Without considering your inner guts.

Whether you are Sad or Glad, Life is taking no Heed of That!

4. If Anything Negative Ever Occurs...

If anything, negative ever occurs,

Immediately change your electro-magnetic course,

Switch your brain's emotional Amygdala

To the front lobes of happiness Gala!

Celebrate every minute of your stay

In the world of no dismay!

Say, "Hurray! "

To a New Day!

Stretch your hand

To everyone on this land!

Say," Hello!"

To every living thing above and below!

Direct your mind

To a conscious mood rewind,

Learn to operate

Your Amygdala's gate!

Become a Star woman / Man

With the mentality of the One!

Deny Yourself the Luxury to React,
Get on the Response Track!

5. Emotional Don'ts

Don't be emotionally flat

Colorless, upset, or sad!

Don't go through life's motion

Without any emotion!

Don't get into a highly toxic set

In your mental faucet!

Don't be a one trip pony

That makes your life ride a phony!

Don't be trapped by life

Without giving someone your five!

Maximize your effort form

On a total self- reform!

This reformation will focus your self-guru

Unapologetically only on you!

Upload your smart phone with the Don't tone!

Learn to Spell Excellence to Remove a Self-Guilt Pestilence!

6. When You Are Completely Forlorn

(An Inspirational Booster)

When you are completely forlorn

Start repeating to yourself on and on, "Come on!

> *Stop sighing and whining,*

> *Start smiling and dining!*

Shake off the lot

Of a depressive thought!

> *Be a spot*

> *Stay aboard!*

Keep going,

Stop moaning!

> *Re-ask yourself fast,*

> *"Am I doing my bit at last?*

What if I die

In a blink of an eye.

> *So much can still be done,*

> *If you are de facto with the God's Son,*

And if you are not the prey

Of many empty words array,

If a true spiritual action

Is your heart-felt reaction,

If you are not dead

To rudeness, rape, or hate, yet!

Then, you are the One

That can't be money-won!

Then, you can see the victory glow

In your new generation's dough.

It's in the eyes of our sons and daughters -

The backup of our new life voters!

So, let's say "Hurray!

To the Indigo Children's way!

Let's help our kids help themselves!

They are born in a new universal cell!

Let them use their smart phone

To structuralize their life's bone!

Step Aside; Let Them Preside!

7. Learn to Resist a Temptation!

Learn to re-

sist

The wimpy "I want it!"

Cyst!

Tell yourself,

"No!"

And calmly

Go

Away from a tempta-

tion

Toward your life's ela-

tion!

When "Yes!" is said, in-

deed

To what you really

Need!

Prefer Needs to Wants to Get Rid of the Soul-Ruining Warts!

8. Weather Whining

Any weather

Is in the God's tether!

Any season

Is for a reason!

You need to accept them, as such

And not to complain that much!

For, if you cannot change the clouds in the sky,

Why would you complain and cry?

Every drop of rain, or a flake of snow

Is the God's way to say Hello!

Smile in response and with gratitude

And without a silly, "Why again?" attitude!

You cannot order God, "More Sun!"

Nor can you demand, "Less rain!" you must sustain!

So, do not mind it,

If you cannot rewind it!

You are a part of the God's weather,

You are in His powerful tether!

It Takes only a Stroke to Change a Minus into a Plus, and So Do It Thus!

The Beauty of Life is Beyond Survive!

"Go Beyond, Fully Beyond, Completely Beyond!" *(The Buddhist mantra)*

9. I'm Never at a Complaint Tether!

I'm never at a complaint tether

About life, health, or weather!

I'm not going to ever beat

The hell out of my boss's nasty meat!

For what's the point to complain,

If you need to sustain, disdain or no disdain!

So, on I go,

Channeling my anger flow,

No matter what,

With or without any one's support!

I live my life, not the boss's or my son's,

Not my friend's or any one's

Whose life is in a tight twine

With an unstable life of mine.

I hardly ask anyone for advice,

For they can't think of my problems twice

Nor can they do that about theirs,

Trying to get to the life's upstairs,

Rushing to find a quick solution

In a personal mind-set pollution.

Every smart   decision

Needs a lot of precision

        To get out of the loop,

        Created by an emotional stoop,

You'd better sit upright

And try to be bright!

        Take a deep breath

        To relax and to decompress

From the pollution

Of a quick problem solution

        Think in the baby steps

        For a positive reflex!

Only those, who never waste

Their mental pace

        Can handle their lives' sense

        Without a hasty negligence!

Also, do not fight

To be always right!

To Be Ever Right, Be Bright!

Section Two

(Step Two   - The Emotional Uplifts – Self-Monitoring)

To Emotionally

Succeed,

Be Language –

Fit!

Be Immune to the Automatic Speaking whims!

Master Your Language Management Skills!

A Woman's Nature is a Puzzle for a Man, Herself, and the Mother Nature's Spell!

(" A Kiss" by Pablo Picasso)

Kiss Wisely and Be Cool; Don't Wear your Heart on the Sleeve like a Fool!

1. Don't You Vent!

Don't you vent and later invent

That you were too emotionally bent!

Who cares, and who can excuse

Your uncontrolled electrical fuse?

That you hit someone with and painfully burn

With your high voltage words, said in return.

An untamed emotional reaction

Is always pregnant with a poignant action!

Your emotional intelligence

Becomes a mere pestilence!

You need to heighten your EQ

To get back into a civil mode's queue!

So, if an emotional urge

Ever occurs,

Burry it then and there

With a cold shower gauze!

Thus, your venting will never bother

A much better EQ of another!

Deny Yourself the Luxury to React, Get on a Response Track!

2. Don't Be Speech-Bubbly!

Don't be speech- bubbly,

Recycle your negatively charged vocabulary!

Clean it of the words of profanity,

Complaining, cursing, and vanity!

Better start reversing

The words of hate into love in rehearsing!

For the true value of the words heard

Is often twisted into a verbal sword!

It can kill, hurt, and injure

More than any other weapon-like danger!

- - - - - - - - - - - - - - - - -

Speaking is an ability to externalize your mental -emotional personality. Artificial language is purely mental.

" If you want to be smart, learn to ask, listen, and answer. Also, stop talking when there's nothing else to say." (Leo Tolstoy)

"First was Word!" It's Written on the Bible's Board!

3. A Sharp Word Wounds Like a Sword!

A sharp word

Wounds like a sword!

It stays in the mind and the heart,

Like a nasty rat!

It bites your emotional tail

And hinders forgetting to no avail

A sword-word

Is, in fact, a bad thought,

Impossible to delete,

Unless you repeat

The God-given bet

To forgive and forget!

So, we need to be bold

To fit in the life's mold!

Only then can we overcome

Bad-mouthed human scum!

Be Always on the Alert for a Sword-Word!

4. Word is Also at the Life's End!

Word is also at the life's end

When the final "Finite a la Comedy! "are said.

True, life is "A Comedy of Errors"

That is reflected in the God's Mirrors

But it would be much less, as such,

If we controlled our words very much!

So, if you don't have something nice to say,

Keep the nasty words at your lips' bay!

Self-Consciousness up-beat is in Being language -fit!

The Fractals of Intellectually Spiritualized Beings:

Form + *Content*

(Body+ Spirit+ Mind) + (Self-Consciousness + Universal Consciousness)

Living Intelligence + *Enlightened Self-Consciousness = A Whole Self!*

Put Your Tongue in the Captivity of the Mind's Run!

5. Get Rid of the Pesky " What If..."!

Worrying about "What if…?

Makes your life freeze and get brief

"What if I don't deliver,

What if I don't have enough silver?

What if he /she cheats,

And I need to detect his / her feats?

What if I get fired,

And never again hired?

What if I get sick,

And my life will never again tick?

What if…? What if…?What if…?

Don't they make your life Stiff?

Stiff with fear and misconception,

Full of regrets and wrong perception

Of yourself and the other,

Stuck in a doubtful "I would rather…"

Why don't we trust ourselves?

Aren't we with God in our mental cells?

"Let go and let God"

Is always in our verbal fort

But do we follow that thought,

Or What?

So, let's get rid of the Ifs

And all our fearful stiffs

Let's trust our guts and God,

To become real masters of our life's fort

For we cannot turn our term on Earth

Into any possible reverse!

Don't ever swoon and howl at the Moon!

Don't apply too much eloquence,

Apply patience and tolerance!

Why Worry for Your Immortal Soul?

God is in Control!

6. To Cool off the Emotional Steam...

(Some more tips on Emotional Diplomacy fits)

To cool off the emotional steam,

Boost up your broken self-esteem!

Say to yourself to self-sustain,

"I am emotionally sane!

I am intelligent and wise

And I can give you some good advice

I can make myself glow

After each hard life's blow

I can treat with some affection

Even the ones , lost in a self-reflection

I bless them and quietly go

Without getting into a fight flow.

I am charming in my own way

Because I can always say

To the evil eye holder,

"Beauty is in the eye of the beholder!"

Then he or she can see me, as such,

Even   though I am not young that much

I need to be invincible in my spirit

Against any unwanted enemy in it!

I need to co-feel and guard

And never ask for an emotional refund!

I need more love to live as long as I can

On the Mother Earth and under the Father Sun!

And I don't want to be evert told

About my imperfect personal mold!

Only then would I make it true

And become an emotional self-guru!

"No matter what happens to you on the emotional plane, do not create more pain for yourself on the mental and spiritual planes.

(Erick Erickson)

Your Life stops Running when You Start Whining!

7. The Motto of My Everyday Life's Show

The motto of my everyday life's show

Is: "Let's go, let's go, let's go!"

But on the aim targeted go,

We shouldn't let anyone run the show!

So, I don't let anybody channel

My mind's or my body's panel!

No one is in charge

Of my life that much!

Only God can show me what I should,

Or shouldn't do without much ado

So," Let God and let go!"

Is the motto of my life's show!

Beauty + Grace + Language Skills

Are My Life-Enhancing Wheels!

Change Your Life's Perception for a Better God's Reception!

8. The Law of the Right Language Use

The law of the right language use

Is in sync with the right behavior fuse

> That we ignite and often abuse
>
> When we are emotionally defused!

Our thoughts result in our words and impact the actions

They, in turn, generate much language fractions.

> That damages our left brains
>
> With the bad habits refrains!

To turn them into good ones

Is impossible to be done at once!

> Patience and Self-Control of a casual language muse
>
> Are required to be put to a regular use!

Tongue accuracy, controlled at a brink,

Demonstrates exactly how we think!

> So, your personal profile brick
>
> Is laid out by the way you speak!

For you and the language in you

Are the inseparable two!

Your Word Might Be a Cutting Sword.

So, Manage Your Word!

Section Three

Step Two- *Love Section of the Emotional Dimension* – ***Self-Monitoring***

Our Ascension

to the

Love Olympus

Upload your smart phone with a lot of love tone!

All the Hearts are Unlocked with One Key – Love!" *(King Solomon)*

" Where There is Love, there is God!"

(Leo Tolstoy)

Pursues and Andromeda

Love Bliss is Not a Myth!

1. Love is Our Spiritual Mold!

Love is encoded in our DNA, and our evolutionary role is to reverse the wrong course that it has taken these days. We are living at the time when *physical attraction is in action while soul connection is in retention!*

Sex Obsession is in Session!

We obviously need <u>to trace our love failures back to the cause</u> and inhabit our souls with a much better *Skills of Self-Growth.* Happiness is based on love, and it cannot be sudden because *love is the process of self-growth in the physical, emotional, mental, spiritual, and universal dimensions.* In the ancient philosophy, love growth is qualified as the stages below, and these stages go hand in hand with the **SPIRITUALIZED SELF-RESURRECTION** that I am trying to promote in my book on love –" **Love Ecology**.".*(www.language-fitness.com)*

<u>The Levels of Love from the Above:</u>

5. Agape *– fraternal Love – Self-Salvation -*   **Universal level**

4. Mania *- love as adoration — Self-Realization -*   **Spiritual level**

3. Sturge *- love as a responsibility - Self-Installation -*   **Mental level**

2. Ludus *- love as a game- Self-Monitoring -*   **Emotional level**

1. Eros *- sensuous love - Self-Awareness*   **Physical Level**

<u>Don't be in a hurry to feel, to love, and to live; Love is a process Still!</u>

Love is a Rainbow of Enlightened Self-Consciousness, though.

2. <u>Don't Be Crowd-Bewitched</u>; Give Love the Freedom of Speech!

(Let's Practice What We Preach)

When we over-rationalize love,

 We get cut off from the Love Above

True love is leaving our guts,

And it's becoming uguts! *(Italian slang for nonsense)*

In the tech era of digital connection,

 We get caught in a disconnection

Of our face-to-face inspection

And a soul-to-soul reflection!

We lose love mentally and emotionally

 Because we expose ourselves only digitally!

Our heart-to-hearts and tete-a-tetes

Happen in hasty superficial fits!

We read the text messages once or twice,

But we don't see the partner's eyes!

Nor do we sigh or romanticize

His or her heart's size!

We are expecting a soul mate,

But we continue to rate

Every one's love track

<u>By the size of his / her money sack!</u>

Nor do we want to commit

To a long-term mutual fit!

> *We break up, make up, or set up,*
>
> *Without thinking twice "What's up?"*

We fall in love with the virtual reality,

Often devoid of human sanity!

> *Hence, love goes in reverse*
>
> *Of its natural human course!*

Men get attracted to handsome males,

Women prefer frailness to real maleness!

> *Is it another case of Sodom and Gomorra,*
>
> *Or should we see it as the saddest "umora"? (Sad laugh in Russian)*

The choices we make, dictate the life we live,

but the Nature's choice is sacred still!

> *And we are not heading to a destruction*
>
> *Of our life-long human function!*

We are just learning to respect love

In the mind and the heart's personal gulf!

> *We need to stop our love over-rationalization*
>
> *And accept or give love without frustration!*

Love without a sex role transmission

May well be a God-given mission!

> *But if the choice is made in a personal net,*
>
> *It's not a free country' business to mess the outlet!*

Love is in the eye of the beholder,

Not in the mass media's molder!

So, be nice and loving and beware

To protect love's eyes and ears everywhere!

May love in you

Preside for the two!

The Fractals of Intellectually Spiritualized Beings:

Form + *Content*

(Body+ Spirit+ Mind) + (Self-Consciousness + Universal Consciousness)

Living Intelligence + *Enlightened Self-Consciousness = A Whole Self!*

The level of a **person's intelligence and his / her self-consciousness** should be in <u>the focus of people's sex orientation</u>, not our judgment and their frustration. Love life is a sacred thing, and **the choices that people make are in them innate.** *Everyone needs to redirect attention to their own perfection and preserve it in bits for our kids! !*

What destroys us is **<u>shamelessness and dirty exposure of sex preferences</u>** that should stay in the space and time of a person's inner twine. Harmony and beauty, kindness and honesty , care and love are the result of a joint work of two people in love in five dimensions, and not to make mistakes in your love choices , **you need to X-ray a person first in the universal, spiritual, mental, emotional ,and finally, physical dimensions.** Then the sex preference would be done without ignorance and negligence!

You are Free to Be the Best of Thee!

3. Spontaneous Sex without Love Shouldn't Be a Regular Stuff!

Spontaneous sex without love

Is nothing but a bluff!

It's like having one glove in sight

On a cold, lonely night!

You cannot get hot or fully perform

In an incomplete uniform!

You remain cold inside

With a wrong partner at your side.

Sex loses its Libido

And becomes a Placebo!

It's like expecting to hear a symphony,

But ending up with listening to a cacophony!

Such sex is very easy to receive,

But it's very hard to self-forgive!

You stop loving yourself

And strive to clean up every memory cell.

Then, you need the sex scene to be remitted,

But find it impossible to be deleted

From the mental rewind

Of your true love's mind

For sex without Love

Is a faked bluff!

We all stop loving

When we are sex- bluffing!

Love shouldn't be faking,

It's must be slowly baking!

"Love is not a Feeling; Love is Action!"

(Willian Shakespeare)

Self-Induction for Love Function:

I Can Roam Any Terrain with Self-Worth in My Vein!

Use technology for your Love Ecology!

Sex without Love is a Bluff!

Energize your Sex with Love!

Learn Loving Without Sex Bluffing!

4." You'd Better Be Alone than with Whoever!" *(Aram Hayami)*

You'd better be alone

That's the true love's role!

> **Being alone**
>
> **You are waiting for your love- clove!**

He or she will appear, no matter what

As your earnestly earned love reward!

> **For, if sex without love is a fake love twin,**
>
> **What's the point of having this self-guilt sin?**

Isn't it better to have some sex fasting

To make your love life longer lasting

> **So, have a love recess**
>
> **Without any sex**

Until you meet the One

Who makes it real fun!

> **And, since in the sex malls,**
>
> **Everything rises and falls,**

Stay in its Happy Beat to feel Lovingly Upbeat!

5. You Are Who You Sleep With!

You are who you sleep with,

And it's not a myth

For we often click with a wrong type,

We tend to be short of our love sight!

Every relationship needs some growth,

It usually falls in sessions with repose.

Nothing that you see in sight

Comes into life over-night!

The same holds true

About a relationship's glue.

Sleeping together is like growing in width, depth, and height

Till real love is at the <u>heart + mind's</u> site!

Otherwise, a quick relationship fix

Is but a fake mix

Of hurry, lust,

And a lot of fuss

About how to gratify

Your selfish thigh!

But if, indeed,

You are in a love-fit,

You'll have to admit

That it's not how you deal with it.

You need to choose the One

Who brings you the inner Sun!

Be the Station for Your Own Love Inspiration!

"Every human contact is a responsibility!"

(Feodor Dostoevsky)

Make your heart smart and the mind kind.

Be One of a kind!

Love Diplomacy hasn't died,

and it Must Be Revived!

6. If You Get Dumped...

If you get dumped and done over with,

You are not a self-love wiz!

Your self-respect gene

Needs much hygiene!

You do not love yourself

The way you are,

And so he or she goes,

"Oh-la-la!"

You fail to obtain your love rights,

And someone controls your emotional sites

You Need to get back

On Your Self-Love track!

And start respecting again

Your time and space vein!

But do not waste your right brain ants

On meaningless one- night stands

Also, stop browsing the Net

For a new Anton or Antoinette!

Just have some love persistence

And practice a" real jerk" resistance

With a new skill in progress ,

You'll never again self-regress

To dumping someone as a disrespectful mode

Of your a progressively going self-corrode!

Learn to love without any restricting conditions,

<u>And mental or monetary inhibitions!</u>

Love that's Not Shared is doomed to be Derailed!

<u>Love that was betrayed gets No Rebate!</u>

(Fortify your Love Fort with an Inspirational Word!

<u>Upload your smart phone with a new love tone!</u>

The Best Love Survey is still to stay away from the Love-Hate Display!

7. Don't Be in a Hurry to Judge!

(A Crush Love Course)

Don't be in a hurry to judge,

It's much better to oblige

> **Your cynic judgement pyramid**
>
> **With a sincere, "This is it!"**

True, there are men,

And there are males,

> **There are women,**
>
> **And there are females**

Who is who?

Is not an easy task to do!

> **But real men,**
>
> **As well as real women's spell**

Are found in abundance

In their inner wonders!

> **So, don't be in a hurry to judge,**
>
> **It's much better to oblige**

Your cynic disbelief

With the sincere, "What if...?"

What if this is the One,

For real, not for fun?

What if I found my soul mate,

My real love or my past love rebate

For the years of the human waste

In a blind love-hate chase?

All I, actually, need

Is to process the One through my inner grid

To be able to simply say

Without a usual dismay,

"He or she is my real bit,

<u>And this is It!</u>"

To learn real love,

Read the book" The State of Love from the Above!

Learn the Art of Seeing with

Your Heart!

Section Four

(Step Two - *The Emotional Uplifts* - ***Self-Monitoring*** *)*

Marriage is an Enigma with a lack of responsibility Stigma!

Body + Spirit + Mind + Self-Consciousness + Super-Consciousness

in sync govern a Happy Marriage's Link!

(For more on love, check out the book "Love Ecology",2020

Love is a Multi-Dimensional Stuff!

Am I a Sworn or an Ugly Duckling?

Beauty is in the Eye of the Beholder.

1. Marriage is an Equation!

Marriage is an emotional equation

Between you and the object of your space invasion!

> *The question, "Who is Who?*
>
> *Remains a ruling sexual guru.*

Either you control me, or I control you,

That's the power of Who!

> *The power for the control*
>
> *Never gets forestalled*

It directs, it invades,

It always breaks!

> *It is a disease*
>
> *Of a de-magnetized "Is!"*

For only the unity of you and me

Constitutes the whole of a love glee

> *So, tap into each other's interface*
>
> *To have an unbreakable love faith!*

Grow into each other's space,

But don't occupy it in a selfish faze!

The trunk of the love's tree

Consists of the two parts, you and me!

One is a minus, the other is the plus,

Both constitute the love mass!

So, who is who?

Is just a puzzle for a guru

For both are inseparable and unbeatable,

And the love between the two is remittable!

I remit your love, you remit mine,

We are both in love twine!

And our emotional health

Shouldn't be a shrink's wealth!

We are both in charge

Of a loving recharge

Of our unified cell

To be able to love-excel!

So, "Seek and you will find"

The match for your heart and the mind!

"A Human Life is based on Three Pillars:

Who to be born by, who to be taught by, and Who to marry!" (Anton Chekhov)

2. Marriage Paradoxes

(A Love Lesson)

One of the marriage paradoxes

That ruins the love match boxes

    And burns the matches of love, one by one, very fast,

    Or does it all at once, just in a blast,

Is the fact that the person you love the most

Often sees you at your absolute worst, as a ghost!

    We hit the brick wall

    In a relationship stall

When we cannot reconcile the partner of a physical heat

With the partner of our originally emotional need!

    The marriage doctrine of meeting each other's needs

    Turns out to sprout the love-hate seeds

Being capricious, selfish, and whining

Kills the urge for a mutual dining.

    The wish to remain exceptional and the Only

    Is wrecked by the one who's always selfish and horney!

Why isn't the habit for a reciprocal intimacy

Being developed from puberty or even infancy?

Why don't we teach our future newly-weds

To have a collective love brain sets -

To take care of the other,

And to cater to one's own mother!

Not to be jittery in their sex needs

And in a hurry to change the love seats!

Then, love in a marriage and marriage in love

Will finally become a real stuff!

And everyone will be able to choreograph

<u>*His or her marriage graph!*</u>

We need <u>to have our exceptionality recognized</u> at the family level of any size!

Unrecognized exceptionality turns into

the complex of inferiority!

A Matrimonial Aura as the Mental Child of both Mates can be preserved Only in Faith!

Love's Bliss is in Every Kiss!

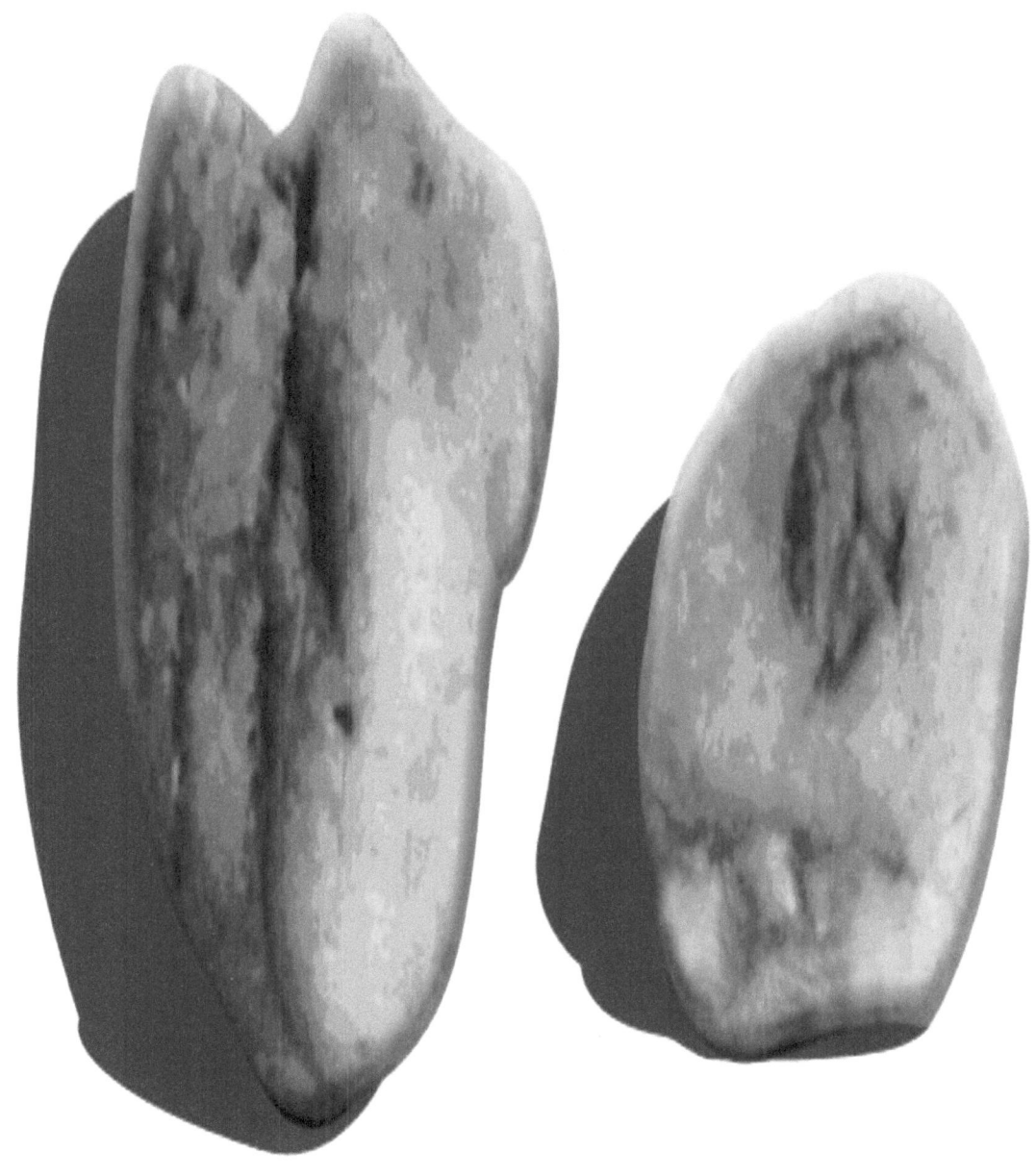

The Resolution of Any Myth is also in a Kiss!

3. To Save Your Marriage's Fate

(A Love Lesson)

To save your marriage's fate,

Get out of your love-hate state!

      Try to get rid of the rows

    Over your intolerance with the marriage wows!

The bi-polar swings of love-hate grins

Can only break your marriage wings

      Stop the competition ado

      Between the two.

For love might cease to fly

And it might die!

      So, keep your hate window sealed

      Against a strong emotional wind!

Also, don't let the lack of money

   Enter you family's door,

      Keep the love window closed

      Don't let it fly afore

For" when poverty enters the door

Love goes through the window, "therefore!

Love is also susceptible to a fight,

Stay away from it, even if you are right!

Each fight is like a match

In a matchbox of a marriage match

It can be burnt, one by one,

During the entire marriage span!

However, one match can sometimes snatch

The entire box, at a touch

Sure, there is no ideal way

To save your marriage from a divorce dismay

But the best survey is still to stay

Away from a love-hate display!

Power up your Mind + Heart to Love and to Be Loved!

Marriage is the ability of the two partners

to share their space and time on the Mutual Love Spine!

"It's not the Laws of Man which Wed Two People, It's always God!" (John Banes)

4. Why Do We Get Divorced?

(The Union of Love is the Holistic Stuff!)

Why do we get divorced,

Or are we at all forced

                To violate the eternal rule

              To be in the spiritual love pool?

For if we click only on the physical level,

Love gets soon ruled by the devil!

              If we click on the emotional sites,

           Love holds on for some time, but it bites!

In case we unite

On the two levels tight,

              When physically, we click,

               And emotionally, we tick,

But mentally, we remain oblique,

Such a connection is still very sick!

               It's only on all the four

                That we are afore!

It's only if we click spiritually

And do it mutually,

We are safe on the mental plane

And, emotionally, we are in gain!

As to the physical clicking,

It'll finally win in seeking!

You'll be a happy mister or miss

And nothing will break the love-bind bliss!

So, why don't we first start with a spiritual love,

Getting the marriage blessings from the Above!

Thus, we'll stop the interior illumination negligence

And obtain true love intelligence!

- -

Marriage from the start to finish and between

is being faithful to the Wedding Ring!

Love is Alive till You Start Moving

Apart in Life!

5. Excessive Kindness is Not Appreciated; It's Money Rated!

Excessive kindness

Isn't appreciated by immature mindlessness

That our kids demonstrate

Once they learn to rate

Life by the money sack

Behind your back!

The hurt from a daughter or a son

Is a life-shortening one!

Raising a child is the greatest chore,

But forming a good human being is even more!

The values that we instill

Reflect our personal self-drill!

If you keep regretting,

Yelling and forgetting

That life in its universal form

Has no de-form,

You'll empty the sack

Behind your back

And you'll have to endure

What we haven't secured!

Excessive kindness is never appreciated,

It's always money- underrated!

So, let the kids learn the hard way

And start to respect your say

Without a superiority scorn,

Instilled by the technological reform.

They still need our supervision

To provide the life-tested reason and vision!

Not to falsely Self-Secure, Don't Lie and Lie-Endure!

" *Modern Psychology has given tacit approval to lying. So, we live in the society based on lies."* (Paul Pearsall)

Every Human Contact is a Responsibility!

6. Focus on Love as Your Mission!

Chose to love who makes you happy at heart

And touches your inner gut,

The one who makes you better for him, or her

To live together, as it's been said before!

Therefore, in a true love mix,

You are who you sleep with!

The connection of minds and eyes,

Not the Thighs

Makes you stretch your hand and unite with the One

Who will become your last One!

So, let's focus on love as our mission

And view it as the path for God's admission!

One morning, Winston Churchill was having a walk with his wife in the park. When they were passing a cleaning man, his wife stopped , greeted the man, and talked to him for some minutes. When Churchill asked her who the man was and why she talked to him, she answered,

"He was my crush in high school. - " You see", reacted Churchill," *if you had married him, you would've been the wife of a street cleaner." –" Oh, No!" –* responded his wife immediately, *"I would've been the wife of the Prime Minister."*

"Behind every successful man is a woman!"

To Complete Each Other, we need to be guided by a Common Goal, rather!

To Balance Yourself,
You Need to Program Your Cells!

The chaos of our past lives is directing us to the order of the present and the future that is mutual!

We are Very Young in the Evolutionary Plan!

7. To <u>Emotionally Survive</u> , Follow the Three Main Rules in Life.

(Spiritual Reminder)

"Reject-Resist - Reform"

(Rabbi Berg / "Taming the Chaos")

Your Love De-form!

To follow God and to be happy in life, no matter what, is not just to be kind, do good things, frequent the church, and pray when life gets sour, but **it also means to tame yourself** <u>physically, emotionally, mentally, spiritually and universally .</u>

Refrain from thinking, saying, feeling, and doing bad things to yourself and others by transforming yourself into a much better human being who never forgets to command to himself / herself,

To Become Your Self-Boss, Don't Reverse Your Self-Worth!

8. Create a Mental Binder for the Inspirational Reminder

Self-Induction for Love-Production:

I Embrace My Love Life

in its Entire Mass

for it Too

Shall Pass!

Use the Auto-Suggestive Meditation for Inner Elation!

(See the Know-How – Section 2)

Love Gravity is based on Love Sanity!

Step One

(Step One - <u>Mind-Sets for the Physical Uplift</u> - **Self-Awareness)**

Look at Life

with a Wonder Glee,

<u>and Just Be!</u>

"Everything must be beautiful in a man - the face, the clothes, the words, and the thoughts."

(Anton Chekhov)

(Self-Induction for Life-Production)

Life-Gaining is in Physical Straining!

Strategize Your Thinking to Actualize Your Mind + Heart Linking!

Step 1 - Be Physically Fit!

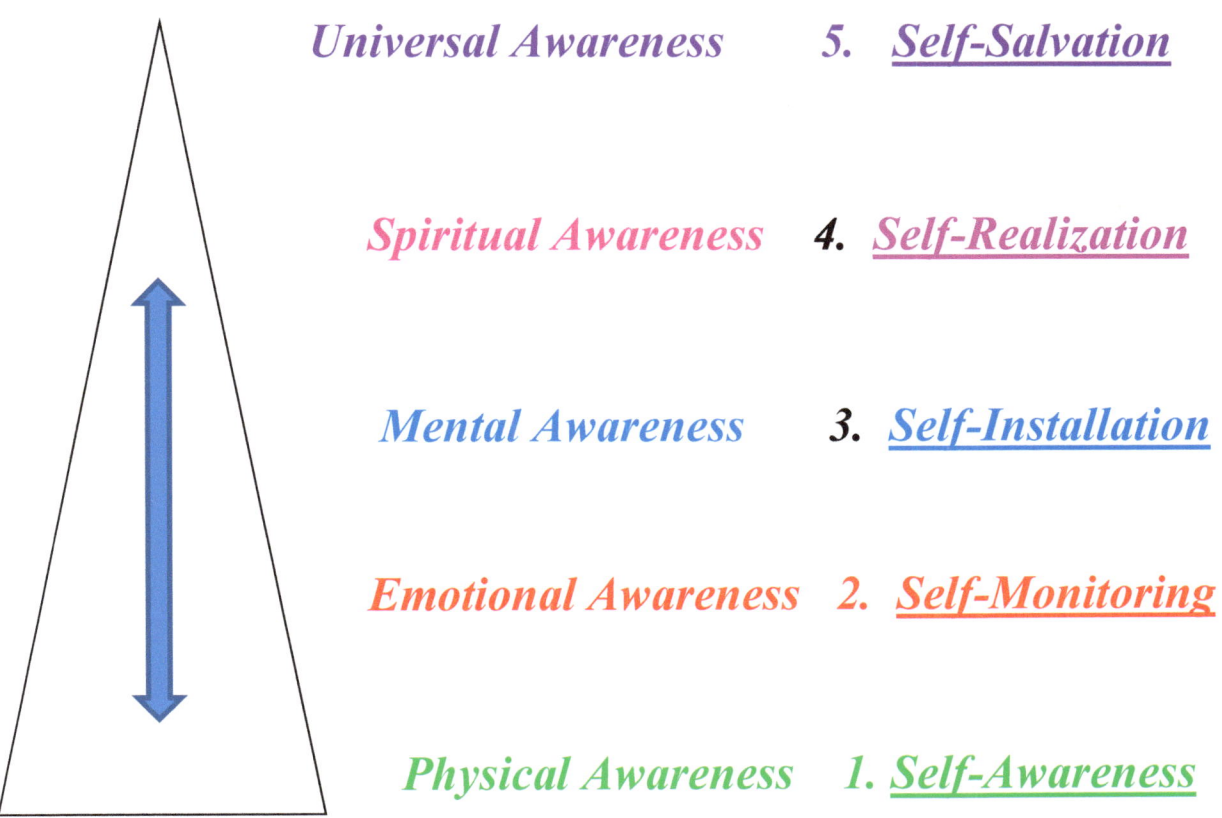

Universal Awareness   5. *Self-Salvation*

Spiritual Awareness   4. *Self-Realization*

Mental Awareness   3. *Self-Installation*

Emotional Awareness   2. *Self-Monitoring*

Physical Awareness   1. *Self-Awareness*

To Be in the Flow of the Life's Fair; Be More Self-Aware!

Start every day with *the victory over laziness, the habit to lie, and the fear to act* by commanding to yourself : *5-4-3-2-1- Launch!* Launch yourself into living with much respect for your life and the desire to obtain self-realization in *the physical, emotional, mental, spiritual, and universal dimensions of life*. Don't live in the simulation of the present and the reflection of the past.

Make your Present Real and Exceptionally Civil!

Section One

(Step One - Mind-Sets for the Physical Uplift - Self-Awareness)

To Better

Self-Repair,

Be More Self-Aware!

"Whoever knows himself, knows God!"

(Muhammad)

To Be in the Flow of the Life's Fair;
Be More Self-Aware!

Am I a Sworn or an Ugly Duckling?

Beauty is in the Eye of the Beholder.

1. I am Unique in Every Stance!

(An Inspirational Booster)

I am unique in every

Stance,

I was born, but only

Once!

There wasn't,

There isn't,

There won't ever be

Anyone like Me!

I am a Life's

Thief;

I want to desperately

Live!

I'm my best friend;

I'm My Beginning and My End!

"To Love Oneself is the Beginning of a Life-Long Romance with Oneself."(Oscar Wilde)

2. God Commands to Self, "*Love Thyself!*"

(An Ode to Self-Efficacy)

If there is no empathy in you

For your mind's guru,

If you do not trust your gut

With a strong regard

For the self-pity and the self-guilt

That often creates your willpower tilt,

You need to bend it toward self-efficacy

That is in you in infancy!

Drive it toward Joseph Campbell's bliss

That is in you has become amiss

Even if you are at the end of the life's tether,

And under the exasperation weather,

Start to put up a fight

With the God-given might

Against any obsession,

Or a self-inflicted depression!

Like a leaf on a tree,

You are absolutely free

To fall off when the wind blows,

Or to sustain the weather foes!

Self-efficacy is the button we push to see

How much lost we are in the human sea!

For we can survive in this human sea,

Only with much self-efficacy!

It is the nature's fee

For the God's empathy!

So, even when you are totally wrong,

Be overly calm and strong!

Do not fall back

On the self-pity track!

So, boost your mind on and on

Without any self-oblivion!

And never get back

On a "Poor me" track!

Remember, everything is perceived in comparison,

A bit of both, bitter and sweet, make your life complete!

Uplift Your Spirit with Every

Passing Minute!

3. Being Perfect is Unrealistic, if Not Sadistic!

Being perfect is unrealistic

And SELF-SADISTIC!

But it's hardly possible,

So, why not try and make your vices reversible?`

Why not stop justifying others and ourselves

And start cleansing your mental spells

That are often self-inflicted

And remain undeleted.

So, place your change waver

In charge of the God's favor!

Life -Gaining is in Self-Taming!

(See the book "Self-Taming!")

Use the Auto-Suggestive Meditation for Inner Elation!

(See the Know-How – Section 2)

Set the Control over Your
God-Given Soul!

4. Not to Lifetime Spare,

Be Holistically Life Direction Aware!

It's hard to get an admission

To the world of competition

Many, it's true

Are better than you!

So, avoid the comparison trap

And be in a unique yourself wrap!

Recognize the reality

Of your self-vanity!

Do not rush to crush

Every rival at the top

Let them drop

With a flop

In the competition

For someone's recognition!

Just wish them well

And continue to self- excel!

Compete only with yourself

In your every cell!

Be better to-day

Than yesterday!

Get smarter today

For a tomorrow's array!

May harmony and balance,

Peace and discipline,

Love and light

Build up your inner might!

Have a Self-Love Zest,

Be the Best!

"It's not enough to Be the Best; Be the Only!"(Steve Jobs)

The Fractals of Intellectually Spiritualized Beings:

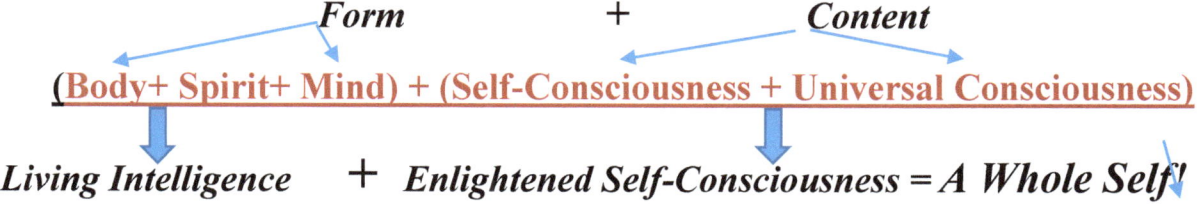

Form   +   Content

(Body+ Spirit+ Mind) + (Self-Consciousness + Universal Consciousness)

Living Intelligence   +   *Enlightened Self-Consciousness = A Whole Self!*

Marvel at the Grander of All and

Self-Install!

5. I'm a Modern Slave in Uncle Sam's Cave!

I'm a modern slave

In Uncle Sam's cave!

I am not as happy as I used to be;

I am a New American Me!

I live under an actionable spell

Of trying hard to excel

At getting my job done

And at paying my bills;

I am striving to cure

My financial ills!

I am rushing and running,

Pushing and driving.

My reckless will

Get s as strong as human steel!

But I am totally alone in this endless spin,

I can hardly change my life's scene.

I survive in my personal cell

Only with God and myself!

There is no one here to really care,

Everyone's full of their own despair!

- - - - - - - - - - - - - - - - - -

I ask myself before I excel,

Can I be rid of this hectic life's spell?

Is everyone here for a wrong reason,

Have we all committed a patriotic treason

Against oneself

And a cherished national cell?

Do we all betray its unique realm

And get drowned in the American Dream's well?

True, the slavery of a hard labor

Turns me into a stereotyped laborer

Stuck in the endless bills

And moderately cheap meals.

I forget myself,

I'm rushing to excel!

For if I don't Opportune,

I'll Sing a "Poor Me" Tune!

6. But I'm a Tough Cookie!

But I'm a tough cookie;

Biting me in two is spooky!

I am sometimes weak, and I demagnetize

My willpower and my inner eyes.

But I can assemble again what's left

Into a whole woman's out- let!

I can stand up not only for myself,

But also, for you, Billy, and for Jeff!

I will always help the one

Who is someone's pathological fun.

I was, I am, and I will be done

With the vices of that clan!

I am a tough cookie,

Biting me in two will be too spooky!

Never Put a Long Face on Your Life's Interface!

7. My Morning Phase

In my morning phase,

As I wash my face,

I stretch my lips in a kind

smile,

And I open up my spirit's

file.

I put on the crown of the queen / king

And try to feel serene!

Then I present myself

To a new day

For a happy life's sur-

vey!

- -

" I don't have everything that I love, but I Love Everything that I have." (Leo Tolstoy)

I Lighten Up and Power Up in My Inner Rehab!

8. No-Victimization = No Frustration!

Non-victimization

Is my life's actualization

> I reduce the victim index
>
> In my DNA matrix!

I never let anyone or the boss

Turn me into a tiny human moth!

> Self- actualization
>
> Is my life's formation

No one can delete

The spark of my divine "It!"

> I stand up at my life's abyss
>
> As a strong, stoical Miss

Who keeps saying to herself and you,

"Don't make much fuss about the life's ado!"

> Being emotionally equipped
>
> I face the life's negative beat!

Shakespeare was not Wrong,

"A Light Heart Lives Long!"

Turn to the Sun to Be Eternally Memorable and Young!

It's Great to Be Embedded in the Humanity's Fate!

9. I Am a Phoenix Bird!

When troubles get

Aboard,

I become a Phoenix

Bird!

I rise from my own

Ashes,

Even after a blow of a

"Fascist!"

I repeat my magic

Word,

"I am a Phoenix

Bird!"

I can rise from the ashes and fly

Again,

I'll just ask God, Where? and

When?

Use the Auto-Suggestive Meditation for Inner Elation!

(See the Know-How – Section 2)

I Never Whine; I Just Shine!

10. Beauty Comes from Within!

Beauty comes from within,

It reflects the world from outside in!

In disciplined thoughts

And beautiful words,

In thoughtful actions

And reserved re actions!

Beauty also comes from outside in,

For those who turn to God from within

Toward   success

In excess

And personal perfection

Under the God's protection!

So be it as it may

On your inner beauty's display!

\- \- \- \- \- \- \- \- \- \- \- \- \- \- \- \- \- \- \- \-

"Be the yard stick of quality."

(Job Steve)

Doing the Right Thing

Gives Your Life a Successful Spin!

11. Be Under Your Own Spell - the Self-Correcting System of the Enlightened Self!

I'm My Best Friend;
I'm My Beginning
And My End!

" My six best doctors are:

Sun, exercise, diet ,

self-confidence, rest, and

<u>friends!</u>"

(Steve Jobs)

Take No Offence - Rely on Your Best Friends!

Section Two

*(**Step One** - Mind-Sets for the   Physical Uplift - **Self-Awareness**)*

Your Character

Formation

is in Life

Elation!

Long Live the Belief in Life

Without " IF !

My Life Paradigm is Still:

I Can ...! I Want to...! And I Will...!

1. Create a Stronger You!

Your character is your habits,

Your virtues and your values!

        They are all the sum of the two

        Your mind and your personality in lieu!

If you have no spirit in you,

You are vague in the mind, too!

        Then your inner guilt trips

        And your many sin slips

Pile in heaps, and all

And your personality gets weak to forestall

        The trials and tribulations

        Of the devil's evil invasion

So, focus on creation a stronger You - Link,

With the mind and personality in sync.

        The mental and emotional parts of two

        Will build up a Much Better You!

Self-Refining is in Self-Redefining!

2. *Just for Today...*

(Manage your day by these   rules every day!)

<u>Just for today</u>

Live through the day,

> *Without tackling at once*
>
> *All the problems in advance!*

<u>Just for today,</u>

Be happy, per say!

> *Even if it does not feel as luck,*
>
> *Be happy, just for a fact!*

<u>Just for today</u>, exercise your spiritual pole

And try to console at least one lost soul!

> *But do not let your kindness be found out,*
>
> *For such announcement does not count!*

<u>Just for today</u>, do two things that you hate,

Without asking for any rebate!

> *<u>Just for today</u>, exercise your willpower say*
>
> *And stick to your word without any delay!*

<u>Just for today</u>, conceal your hurt feelings,

Or your pitiful wrong dealings

For who dares,

And who really cares

To poke into the display

Of your broken spirit's array?

Just for today, try to be agreeable

Even to the most unforeseeable!

Keep your voice low

And criticize not a foe,

For he / she is not the only defect

In the world's web imperfect!

Just for today,

Look beautiful at the work's bay,

Dress becomingly

And talk business-mindedly,

For being courteous and having manners

Is what overly matters!

Just for today, put the two pests,

Hurry and indecision, at rest!

Just for today, communicate with your boss,

Without being a sugar- coating moth!

Just for today, *have a quiet half hour*

To regain your inner self-power!

Just for today, do not fret

What's not out there properly set

Just for today, accept life, as such,

And give the world the best of you, that much!

To finally enjoy your life under the Sun

As the God-given time-limited Fun!

Every month on full moon, **DO SELF-SCANNING** and **SELF-ASSESSING** *in five levels of life - physical, emotional, mental, spiritual, and universal.* (*See the books on Self-Resurrection below*) *Developing yourself holistically, you'll manage to get rid of your pesky bad habits that continuously generate problems for you.*

BE OBJECTIVE *and honest. If you do it during at least three months of the year, by the end of each year, you'll be* **BETTER INSIDE AND OUTSIDE,** *and you'll make, yourself and others happier.*

Be Full of Vim, Vigor, and Vitality -

Zest, Zeal, and Zenith Mentality!

Set up Simple Goals to Deal with Each Day's Problem Moles.

3. Fear Reduction is Your Main Character Function!

Don't Life-Fear,

Life-Steer!

"Reject, Resist, and Reform"

Any Fear Deform!

Use the Auto-Suggestive Meditation for Inner Elation!

(See the Know-How Part – Section 2)

Self-Induction:

I Can Roam Any Terrain with God in My Vein!

Be a Human Angel!

Angels Fly because They Take Themselves Lightly!

4. He Died the Most Meaningful of Deaths!

(Written on the day of Michael Jackson's untimely death)

He died the most meaningful of deaths

That brings the pain full of test to millions abreast!

His music pierces the hearts

And salts the wounds

Of those who have got the eyes

And marvel at his moves!

His energy and inner quest

Were God's perfection, synchronized with zest!

He magnetized the mob,

But never was a snob!

He sharpened up the blade

Of our most entertaining trade

To such a shape

That no one can ever duplicate

The pop perfection of his rate!

Let's Keep Michael's Happy Beat And Be Exceptionally Upbeat!

5. If You Rest, You'll Rust!

If you rest,

You'll rust, very fast!

You'll lose my agility

And my unique masculinity / femininity.

You'll get sloppy and sluggish ,

And you'll become a human gabbage

That is heavy to carry,

Unless you remarry!

Rustiness, like laziness,

Is a pure craziness!

It puts you out of the cart

And you become retard!

So, learn to live consciously

And love more graciously

To finally deserve

To be spiritually preserved!

Make Your Mental Wings Blow off Your Emotional Swings!

Section Three -

*(Step One - Self-Induction for Age Reduction - **Self-Awareness**)*

Defy the Gravity

Of Your Age;

Be a _Self_ -Sage!

Any Age is the Soul's Base!

I'm in (January, May, July, October , and December) of my life,

I Am Alive!

My Life is Going on,

And It's Great in Any Age Form!

The Bliss of Life is at the Sunrise of Passion and the Sunset of Compassion!

(Pictures by Igor Irman)

An Old Age Bliss is Not a Myth!

1. I am 27 and Not a Day More!

(A Self- Rejuvenating Booster)

I am 27 …,

    and not a day more,

I am as young as ever

    before!

        I am dynamic,

        As ever,

        I am sluggish -

        Never!

I was,

    I am,

And I will be

    Young

F-o-r-e-v-e-r!!!

Say this booster, looking at yourself in the mirror

. Upload it into your smart phone to keep up your young spirit's tone!

"It's not Years in Your Life that Matter;

It's Life in your Years!"

2. Defy the Gravity of Your Age; Be a Self-Sage!

(A Booster for old Age Resistance)

Defy the gravity of your

age

With a graceful

rage!

Meet it with the

Charm

Of a totally irresistible

Femme / man!

Live in the tri-

nity

Of love, light, and infi-

nity!

You are the One who Makes you Young!

Transform Your Age into Self-Vintage!

3. I am 50-Something...

I am 50-something,

But I am still life-bursting

I am still going up the hill,

I have a lot of emotional stuff to heal!

I still need to forget and to forgive

To thank, to receive, and to give!

The emotional clutter that I possess

Still needs the cleaning of its excess!

My mental lay-out

Needs a new rebound!

Is all this stuff

A young person's bluff?

Maybe, I need a re-birth

Of my own self-worth?

Maybe I need to re-live

The love that I still feel.

Maybe, I need to rebuild

My poorly constructed life field?

Isn't it what we all need,

Without paying to age much heed.

So, let's not hurry to descend,

We'd better continue to ascend

The higher, the better

That's the evolution of the human matter!

Up there, we'll all meet again

In the unanswerable When?!

- - - - - - - - - - - - - - - - -

Don't be lazy, when getting old.

Remain spunky and bold!

Every Age Season is a Blessing for a Reason!

Use the Auto-Suggestive Meditation for Inner Elation!

(See the Know-How Part – Section 2)

"God helps those who help themselves"

to go beyond their Limited Spells!

4. I Reserve Myself for a Longer Life's Cell!

On the day of my 62,

I reconsidered my age, like a self-guru!

I reversed myself

Into a young woman's / man's cell!

I switched the gear

For another love-making year!

I broke my mold of the old,

I made myself young and bold!

My stature is straight,

My skin is great,

My brain is in touch,

I am still a catch!

I cannot afford

To be an old fart!

I need to take care of myself in sync

Because men see much better than they can think!

I still need

To be in heat,

To please and to release

The need to be at peace!

No, I am not dead

I am not old, yet!

- - - - - - - - - - - - - -

Life is not over when you age;

You just need to become a wise sage!

Use technology for Self-Ecology!

(Upload your smart phone with a rejuvenating tone!)

Everything I Have, I Do, I See

Gladdens Me!

5. The Last Love's Bite

When we turn seventy

Life becomes a confettie

We do not need to bite

Life at the side!

We can love again

And feel love in its stem!

Love becomes age resistant,

And it makes sex persistent

We do not worry over its being folly,

We feel it to its true core, and no more!

We, finally, enjoy the life's bliss

At its autumn striptease!

We start smiling at the clouds,

And we stop being in doubts

That we're going live and love again

In the unanswerable when!

So, to live that long

Preserve your spiritual form

And bless every day's site

For the last love bite!

Live and Love while You are Alive!

Section Four

*(**Step One** - Mind-Sets for the Physical Uplift - **Self-Awareness**)*

Love Life
in its Entire Form;
It's Your Physical
Uniform!

Open Your Mouth for the Life-Wonder Wows!

The First Step in Sight is the Life's Tested Might!

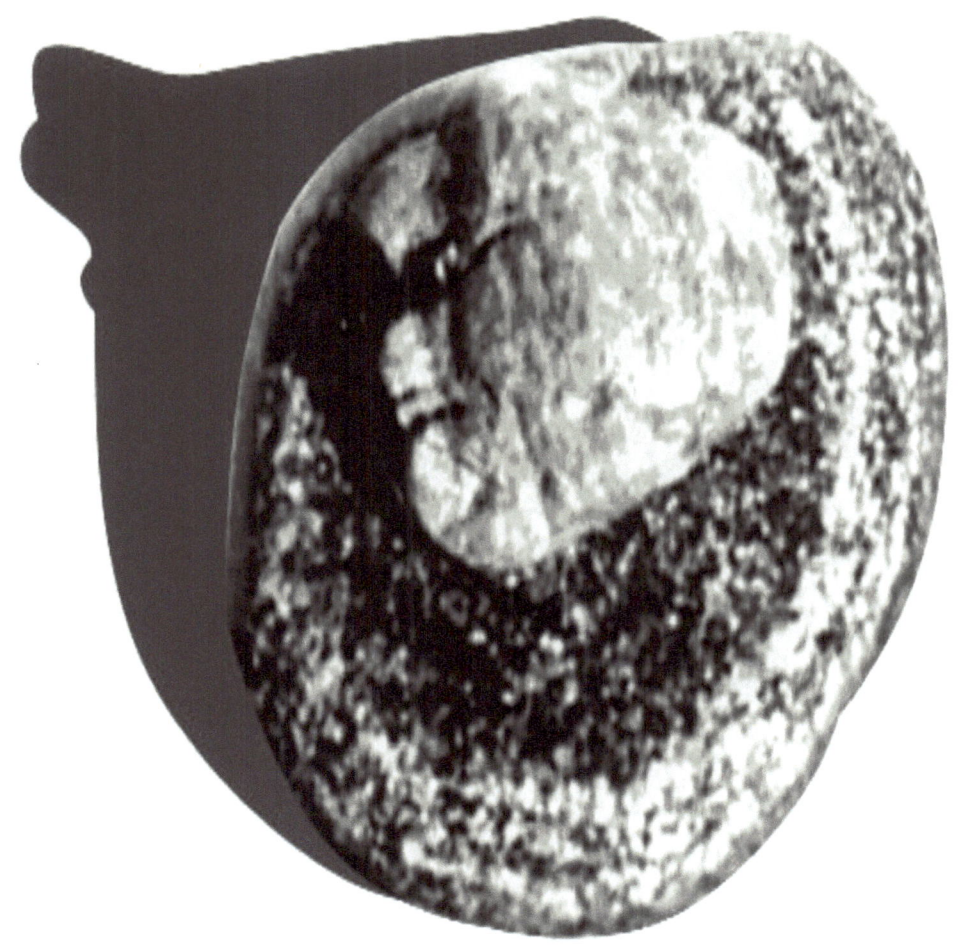

Happiness is Not a Reward; it's the consequence of your stepping forward!

1. Wow! Some Day is Now!

Wow!

Some day is Now!

Not tomorrow, not in a month,

Next year, or as soon as…

Every day hits but once,

And it gives you a chance

To do what you have postponed

And inwardly toned

With a yarning vexation

For your unjustified procrastination!

There is no way to stop the clock

From ticking in the life flock!

Space the time and time the space

Of your personal life's interface!

So, if you are irritable and life unfit,

Immediately snap out of it!

"Follow the Bliss" of the Uncatchable IS!

2. Life is Beautiful and Infinite!

Life is beautiful and in

finite,

Master it to be happy

In it!

For if you don't master it,

It'll master You,

And you'll become a life's

slave,

Not your life's

guru!

Managing yourself inside

Is the priority of your life!

"The Best is Yet to Come"

(Carolyn Leigh)

Take Every Life's Low Tide

in Stride!

3. I'm a Part of the Mother Nature!

I am a part of the Mother Nature,

I have it in me, as my second nature!

I love its stillness and the storm,

I enjoy the weather in its every form!

I admire the shapely clouds,

I try to decipher their tricky bows

I belong to the God's domain,

I am in His cosmic main!

I am in every drop of the rain,

I am in every ray of the Sun,

I am inseparable in my brain

With the God and His Son!

I am in unity

With the divine sanctity!

"Above all else, guard your heart, for it is

the wellspring of life." (Proverb 4:20)

I am a Life Cell; I am Life itself!

4. I Love Life in its Every Shape!

I love life in its every shape,

<u>*I marvel at an ant, a bird, and an ape.*</u>

Every life cell has been reborn

For millions of years, on and on.

The main resource

Is always in force

We can never delete

Its mighty wit!

So, stay in awe,

Life is afore!

Don't push it back

On a waiting track!

Every minute, every hour

Is for you to devour!

So, keep seeing, start feeling,

Keep hearing, stop fearing!

Live life and receive

If you perceive

The God's every smile

In your life's twine.

It may be very coarse,

<u>*But do not change its mighty course!*</u>

<u>Live on, of course!</u>

Change yourself while you are young, not to be confined to the two banal maxima - to eat tastefully and sleep restfully.

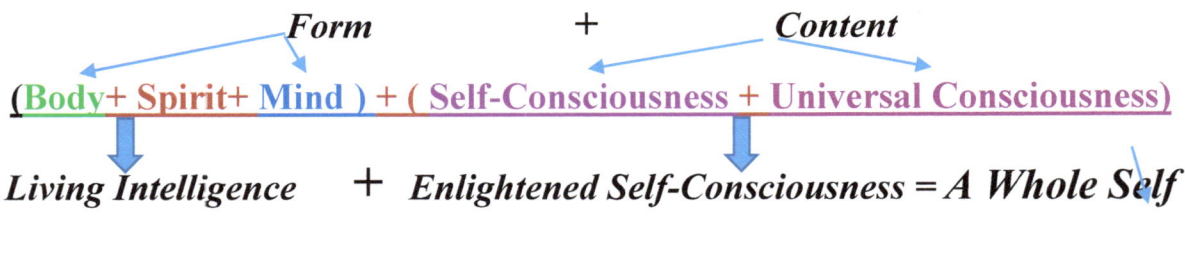

<u>The Fractal of Intellectually Spiritualized You:</u>

Form + **Content**

(<u>Body</u>+ <u>Spirit</u>+ <u>Mind</u>) + (<u>Self-Consciousness</u> + <u>Universal Consciousness</u>)

Living Intelligence + *Enlightened Self-Consciousness* = *A Whole Self*

"God's ultimate goal for your Life on Earth is not comfort, but Mind and Character development."

(Albert Einstein)

Boost Your Life Every Day,

<u>but Most Often - Today!</u>

5. A Bee Lesson

I am a God-designed bee

To produce the life's honey!

I am a scrupulous worker,

I am not a wasteful talker!

I fly for miles in a hurry

To pick up ounces of honey

I get through a very narrow way

Doing my every flower's survey.

I am a part of the bees' system kit,

I never go astray to resist it!

I discipline my fee

To the call of the Mother bee

The outcome of my hard toil

Is never bitter or spoilt

I collect my sweet delight

In the try of my every flight

So, let's gain some insight from a bee-lesson's might

And never get idle or sour inside!

Devote Your Lifetime to Self-Refining!

6. A Mechanical Outburst

(A Car's Confession is in Session)

My car goes forth

In its mechanical outburst!

"I am a Toyota 396,

I am the Sun-lit Pegasus!

I ride through any terrain

Of a man-built domain

When you are driving me,

I am glowing with my mechanical glee

I follow your every touch,

I love you so much!

Who said that a mechanical thing

Can't have an emotional fling?

Every car has a sex drive,

It's at the grip of the buyer's five!

If a man buys a car,

It becomes his best woman from afar

For a woman, a car is a protection wall

To be able to weather and to forestall

The winds and the rains

Of many unknown life terrains!

Your car, as a body kind,

Embodies your matter and your mind!

So, enliven and personalize

Both its motor and its size

So, drive it respectfully, not for fun,

You and your car are One!

Stay overly connected! Disconnectedness is Death!

A Joke with a Message

A man was driving fast on the highway, talking on his phone. Suddenly, he noticed a huge slogan on the side of a church that he was passing by.

- " Stop to say" Hello" to Jesus Christ. Keep driving and texting if you want to see Him in person!"

Make Every Driving Decision with a Lot of Precision!

7. I'm Giving Birth to a New Human Universe!

(A Young Mother's Confession in giving life procession)

I'm giving birth

<u>To a new life in re-birth!</u>

> I'm like the Mother Earth,
>
> I'm its life-giving Force!

While my fruit is ripening in me,

I need to better see

> How and where to let my seed grow
>
> To be able to plant it on the success go.

I want my son, or maybe, daughter,

To be strong and fly above the water

> Like a Pegasus in the sky,
>
> He / she will call me from there, "Mom, I can fly!"

So, let's read into the clouds' hazy shapes,

<u>They are the language of our fates!</u>

Venturing into the Unknown, Our Kids are accomplishing the Goals of Their Own!

8. The Spring of My Heart and Mind

The spring of my heart and mind

Is now in a full bloom to rewind.

My past emotional knots

To let me remove the present-day warts

The spring of my up-lifted butt

Breaks up into new flowers at heart!

New fresh ideas, actions and hopes

That helps me transform my inner mopes

And break into a smiley face

Of my even-unbroken faith

Till the final release

Of my appreciation of what Is!

With the mission accomplished in East!

I can finally depart

Without any regrets,

But with many finished bets!

- - - - - - - - - - - - - - - - - - -

"Change Your Responses to What Happens

To You in Life" (Antony Robins)

The Sunset of an Accomplished Life!

Закат над озером лотосов

Don't Just Survive!
Enjoy the Triumph of Your Life!

Section Five

(Step One - Mind-Sets for the Physical Uplift - Self-Awareness)

I'm Happy,
No Matter What!
Happiness is
My Full-Time Job!

Induct Yourself with Happiness Hygiene.

It's Your Inner Gene!

"If You Want to Be Happy, Just Be,"

Like God and Me!

1. I am God to Myself!

I am God to myself

And to my every cell -

To my mind and my heart,

To my liver and the gut,

To every tiny curve's way

In my brain's grey matter display!

I am the boss

When I am in wrath.

I am the queen,

When I am serene!

I am the one who channels my every cell

To the Mt. Sinai of self-excel!

I am in charge

Of my every cell's surcharge!

I generate, I obligate, I manage, I dismiss,

I am my life's Mister / Miss!

I am the maker of my life,

I am the woman / man of Steve Job's type!

Life is Going on, and it's Beautiful in My Own Form!

2. Help Me, God, Feel Big!

Give me five, to say the least,

It'll make the world of difference!

   Help me, God, feel big,

   Give me a strong twig!

Uplift me to the New Worlds,

I'll sing the panegyric to You in words!

  In the 7th Heaven of my self-belief,

  I can do whatever without If!

I'm totally equipped

To get my life's uplift!

Use the Auto-Suggestive Meditation for Inner Elation!

(See the Know-How – Section 2)

Long Live the Belief in Myself
Without "If"!

3. The Way We Live Determines the Way We Die!

The way we live

Determines the way we die

Many as the earth fertilizer,

Some that are much wiser

Remain above the Earth

For a new spiritual rebirth!

The ideas of every genius's quest

Fill up the atmosphere's fest!

They later sprout in the heads of the best

That are not mentally at rest.

We know, but we are not aware

How it is done and where?

How do we reincarnate,

Or how does the universe ornate

A man, as a worthy one,

To join back the human clan?

How clean

Is one supposed to be of his / her sin?

Do we have another chance

On the universal life stance?

What if I cannot perfect

Even a single defect?

For sure, not to be a fertilizer,

I must become much wiser

To live more consciously,

And to love much more graciously.

Then, I could finally deserve

To be spiritually preserved!

"Please, forgive me, Earth, for having left you."

(The final words of the main character from the Russian rock-opera "Yunona and Avos.")

Face the Sun not to be in the shadow of the Life's Fun!

Don't Ever Die with the Music still
Present in Your Thigh!

4. Face the Sun Not to Be Emotionally Overrun by any Trouble or Fun!

Always face the Sun,

Not to be emotionally over run!

For when you face the sun rays crew,

The shadows fall right behind you!

But if you hide from the light,

The shadows will fall inside!

In fact, what you bravely face

Gets proven by your strong faith,

But what you hide from and ignore

Comes biting you back, as before!

It destroys your personal mast

With the shadows of the past!

So, face the Sun

And enjoy its light giving fun!

Even the God's only Son

Was always praying, facing the Sun!

This Advice is Always Apt.

So, Act!

5. Take Life as a Reward!

Take your life

 Without any strife!

 It might not be fair,

 But it's temporarily affair!

So, whole-heartedly ac-

 cept

Its God-given con-

 cept

 That you need to practice detach-

 ment

 From any evil attach-

 ment

To anyone or anything

That ruins the sync

 Between you and God,

 And life as a God-given reward!

Do Not Speed down the Highway of Your Life's Ride; Take it in Stride!

6. "Time is Not Money; Time is Life!"

(Sadhguru)

Live your life consciously and

Without a frown,

Try to slow up

Your slow down!

Be Happy with your life's

Seat

And your heartbeat

In it!

Accept Life in its entire

Mass,

For It Too Shall

Pass!

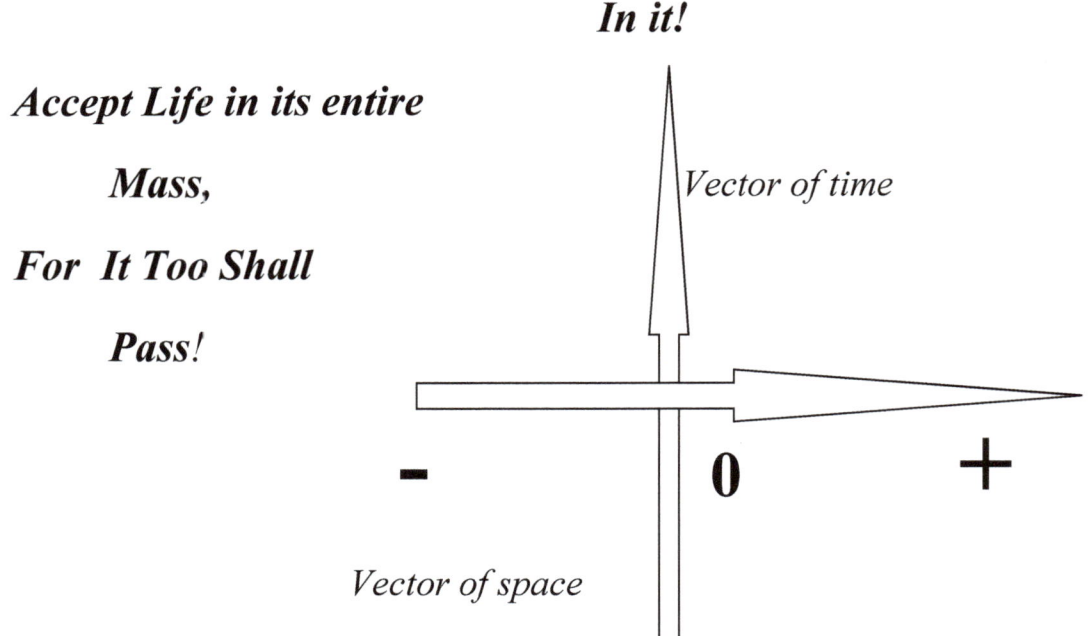

Learn to Life-Shine in Space and Time!

7. To Self-Refine, Give Time to Time!

Some more mind-sets to inspire and sadness to rewire!

1. *Every beginning is 80% of the outcome, if well-done!*

2. Endorphin and serotonin are in the happiness gene.

3. Sleep tight to have the life might!

4. Napping helps in trouble-gapping.

5. *Make the rule of life - No bitter strife!*

6. Don't give a gift of love to a poor souled dove!

7. Be picky in love and the food stuff!

8. "Every relationship ends - the question is when and how."

9. *Monitor the stress without any fear mess!*

10. Laughter fills the soul with the cleansing foam!

11. Smile to everyone and everywhere to conflict -beware!

12. If you want to be wise, don't hurt anyone with your vice!

13. *Be rich in the soul to beat any money-channeled goal!*

14. Don't compete and compare. be the best here and the!

15. Don't envy anyone, yet. Every sunrise has a sunset!

Don't Be Live-Negligent; Be Life-Intelligent!

8. To *Physically Survive* , Follow the Three Main Rules in Life.

(Spiritual Reminder)

"Reject-Resist - Reform"

(Rabbi Berg / "Taming the Chaos")

Your Inner De-form!

To follow God and to be happy in life, no matter what, is not just to be kind, do good things, frequent the church, and pray when life gets sour, but **it also means to tame yourself** **physically, emotionally, mentally, spiritually and universally.**

 Refrain from thinking, saying, feeling, and doing bad things to yourself and others by transforming yourself into a much better human being who never forgets to command to himself,

Give up Your Self-Negligence,

Become the Living Intelligence!

(Check out the Excellence Award winning book, 2020, ***"Living Intelligence or the Art of Becoming!"****- www.language-fitness.com)*

9. Create a Mental Binder for the Inspirational Reminder:

Self-Induction for Life -Production:

I Embrace My Life

in its Entire Mass

for it Too

Shall Pass!

Use the Auto-Suggestive Meditation for Inner Elation!

(See the Know-How Part – Section 2)

Life is Me;

Life is My Philosophy!

Don't Ever Swoon and Howl at the Moon!

(The Tree of Life)

Water Your Tree of Life with the Inspiration Glee and Just BE!

Conclusion of Self-Infusion

Happiness
is the Feeling of
Wholeness!

The Fractals of Intellectually Spiritualized Beings:

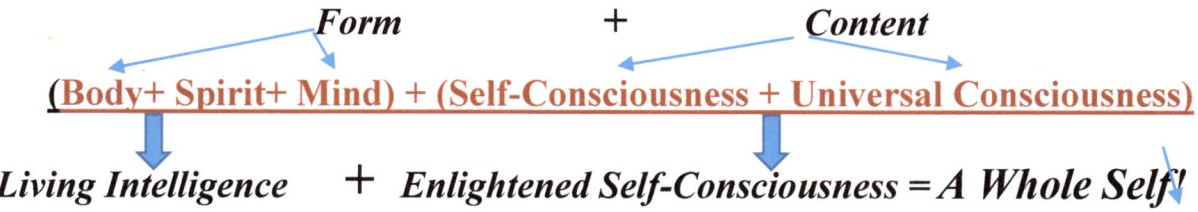

Form + *Content*

(Body+ Spirit+ Mind) + (Self-Consciousness + Universal Consciousness)

Living Intelligence + *Enlightened Self-Consciousness = A Whole Self!*

The Form and Content of Life in Sync
Form the Universal Link!

1. *Self-Perfection is the Way to Self-Resurrection!*

The Matrix of a Personality Formation:

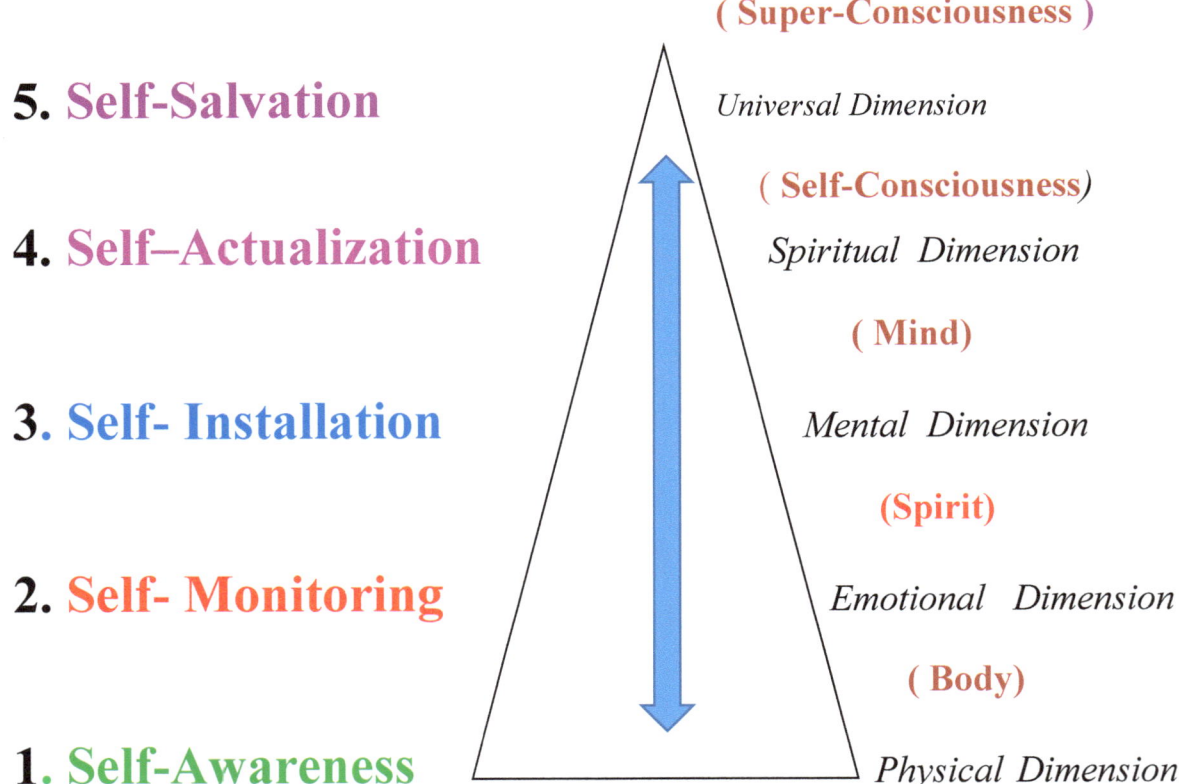

5. Self-Salvation

4. Self–Actualization

3. Self- Installation

2. Self- Monitoring

1. Self-Awareness

(Super-Consciousness)

Universal Dimension

(Self-Consciousness)

Spiritual Dimension

(Mind)

Mental Dimension

(Spirit)

Emotional Dimension

(Body)

Physical Dimension

The Spiritual Fractals of Being:

Body + Spirit + Mind + Self-Consciousness + Universal Consciousness =

A Soul-Refined Self!

I have pinpointed here the way of performing self-change and self-growth, not as a dictator, but as an instructor who had verified this way with hundreds of students that got self-inspired and self-transformed with this vision installed. *Visualize this route to sustain it in any mood!*

Self-Salvation is in Our Spiritual Maturation!

2. Infuse Your Self-Realization Fuse!

Be more mature

On your universal life's tour!

        Take the responsibility

        For your action's disability!

For all the steps you take

Have the consequences at make!

        They are engraved at your birth

        In the action plan of the Universe!

So, take a guess and see

What the reaction could be

        But try to see the result in advance,

        And do it always, not once!

Remember, the Law of Cause and Effect

Is permanently in effect!

        And if you want to hit the goal,

        Do the surgery of your soul!

Fill up your digital mind

With live cells ready to unwind

The Double Helix of an Animal DNA into

the Five-Dimensional Star Man's Display!

3. Our Universal Happiness Seam is in the Time-Space Beam

The universal happiness in the time-space beam

Is not just Einstein's utopian dream!

Why isn't it possible for us to accept

That we haven't ruled the world from the outset.

Aren't we able to fully perceive

The scope of hatred that we receive.

Why don't you feel for an Afghan mother

Who has the same blood as any other,

And whose religious stem

Is much stronger than that of Uncle Sam!

Off we should go,

And let the other nations know

That we want them to further glow

In accordance with the universal flow!

"Live and let Live!"

Should be the entire world's belief!

Our brave soldiers, for sure, know

What is what?

But are they free to retort, Or what?

Why don't we then call

Upon the entire world's military recall

To have hands off Iraq, Syria, Afghanistan,

Israel, Palestine, Yemen, or Pakistan!

Let's stay where we belong

And try to truthfully perform

What the people expect

Their President's role to perfect!

With the mission accomplished,

Let's help to construct

What we've destroyed

With our democracy declaration act!

Only then will the universal happiness rein

On every country's unique terrain!

And the eternal peace in the time-space beam

Will stop being Einstein's Utopian Dream!

May our Human Essence Obtain True
Spiritual Renaissance!

4. Conscious Self-Scanning is Life - Refining!

In conclusion, life is the time-space process, not an immediate result, and to monitor this process successfully, we need to inspire ourselves for life every minute, never forgetting that our visit on the planet Earth is temporary.

To have the life in control, do **CONSCIOUS SELF-SCANNING** daily, raise your *self-awareness, enrich self-knowledge, and fortify self-love.* Get in the habit of boosting your spirit with every accomplishment at the *mini, meta, mezzo, macro, and super levels* of your personality-formation and self-creation. This is what this book is all about and, hopefully, it has helped you to better yourself to be able to declare.

To get more Life-Fit, learn to admit:

I admit, *I'm Physically Fit.*

I admit, *I'm Emotionally Fit.*

I admit, *I'm Mentally Fit.*

I admit, *I'm Spiritually Fit.*

I admit, *I'm Universally Fit!*

(For more ,see the book " Beyond theTterrestrial1")

I'm a Whole Me,

I'm the Best I Could Ever Be!

Structural Perfection is in Every Life's Section!

Order and Love generate Your Inner Beauty's Stuff!

Post Word

(As the Final Award!)

More Mind-Sets

Against

Up-Sets!

Remember,

"The happier you behave, the less upset you get!"

(Paul Pearsall)

Self-Induction for Life -Production:

I Never Whine or Life Frown,

"I Slow Up My Slow Down!"

1. To Live Long, Get Psychologically Strong!

1. Work on your conscious living,

Being, becoming, and perceiving!

2. Remember, every good

Takes time and a good mood!

3. To stay always life-obsessed

Gets your excessive happiness processed!

4. Be immune to depression,

Self-pity ,anger, and aggression!

5. Release your worries into God's hands,

Solutions are His magic wands!

6. Thinking is a magnet,

Whatever you project, you gonna get!

7. Psychology is often at a service of the one

Whose mind is totally blind,

And the heart is not too smart.

Only you can put an end to that!

8. Avoid being judgmental of the other's moral cell,

Pay more attention to yourself!

9. Don't live closing your eyes to the future

And burying your head in the past,

You are going to pass the present fast!

10. When you are bettering yourself,

Don't bitter your cells!

11. Drive your mental mobile alone,

Don't let anyone or anything,

Drugs or meds,

Narrow down your brain's outlets!

12. Have an inner seal

Of your determination steel!

13. Deny yourself the luxury to react,

Get on the response track!

14. Touching your pulse,

Feel your life without any farce!

15. Get rid of the "either or" mentality

Better act decisively on the "both and" unity!

16. Change your hate mood

Into the love brain food!

Avoid a Comparison Trap; Be in the Unique Yourself Wrap!

2. Inner Peace is the Aristocracy of the Spirit. Be "Ageless and Timeless" in it.

(*Deepak Chopra*)

Orchestrate the Symphony of Love

in your mind,

Conduct the Music of Thought

in your heart,

And Be Overly Happy,

doing that!

ke Your Heart Smart and the Mind Kind; Be One of a Kind!

3 Life is Going on; Make it Happy in Your Own Form!

Long Live the

Beat of

"So Be It!

Life is a road test. So, don't protest!

Accept it as such and be happy very much!

Rule Your Life to Confidently Thrive!

Life is Tough, but I'm Tougher!

I Can Roam Any Terrain with Faith and Confidence in My Vein!

Give the Gift of Yourself to the Universal Life's Cell!

Openly Smile to prolong your Life's Worthwhile!

The title page design is by Yolanta Lensky
(yolanta HYPERLINK "mailto:3699@gmail.com" Yolanta3699@gmail.com)
The pictures of the rocks and other pictures are from Dr. Ray's personal collection

Check the video in the Self-Resurrection section at
WWW.LANGUAGE-FITNESS.COM

Give the Gift of Yourself to the Universal Life's Cell!

Openly Smile

to prolong

your Life's

Worthwhile!

The title page design is by Yolanta Lensky

(yolanta HYPERLINK "mailto:3699@gmail.com" Yolanta3699@gmail.com)

The pictures of the rocks and other pictures are from Dr. Ray's personal collection

Check the video in the Self-Resurrection section at

WWW.LANGUAGE-FITNESS.COM